Structured Exercises in

Management

Volume

2

Structured Exercises in

Management

A Handbook for
Trainers, Educators, Group Leaders

Volume

2

Edited by
Nancy Loving Tubesing, EdD
Donald A Tubesing, MDiv, PhD

REPRODUCTION POLICY

Library of Congress Cataloging in Publication Data

Structured exercises in stress management : A handbook for trainers, educators, and group leaders / Nancy Loving Tubesing and Donald A. Tubesing, eds.
192p. 23cm.
Summary: A collection of thirty-six exercises for stress management to be used by trainers and facilitators in group settings.
ISBN 1-57025-015-4 (v.2 : pbk) : $29.95
1. Stress (psychology)—Prevention, problems, exercises, etc. 2. Stress—Psychological, prevention & control, problems. I. Title. II. Tubesing, Nancy Loving III. Tubesing, Donald A.
BF575.S75S74   1984, 1988, 1994
158'.92—dc19   83-61073

Printed in the United States of America

10 9 8 7 6 5 4 3 2 1

Published by:

WHOLE PERSON ASSOCIATES
210 West Michigan
Duluth MN 55802
(800) 247-6789

PREFACE

Over a decade ago we launched an experiment in health education—the Whole Person series of **Structured Exercises in Stress Management** *and* **Structured Exercises in Wellness Promotion**. *We believed that it was time to move beyond peptalks and handouts to an experiential approach that actively involves the participant—as a whole person—in the learning process.*

What began as an experiment has become a catalyst for dramatic changes in health promotion and education! **Structured Exercises** *volumes have found their way into the libraries of trainers, consultants, group workers, and health professionals around the world. We're proud that these volumes have become classics—the resource of choice for planning stress management and wellness promotion programs.*

Our purpose in publishing this series was to foster inter-professional networking and to provide a framework though which we can all share our most effective ideas with each other. As you will soon discover, we scoured the country looking for the most innovative, effective teaching designs used by the most creative consultants and trainers in business, health care and social services, then included some of their most imaginative ideas in this volume.

Many of the exercises we designed ourselves and refined in hundreds of workshops we've conducted over the past twenty years. Some are new combinations of time-tested group process activities. Others were submitted by people like you who continually strive to add the creative touch to their teaching.

The layout of **Structured Exercises** *is designed for easy photocopying of worksheets, handouts and preparation notes. Please take advantage of our generous policy for reproduction—but also please be fair to the creative individuals who have so generously shared their ideas with you.*

☞ *You may duplicate worksheets and handouts for use in training or educational events—as long as you use the proper citation as indicated on the copyright page. Please also give written credit to the original contributor. Whenever we've been able to track down the source of an idea, we've noted it. Please do the same when you share these ideas with others.*

☞ *However, all materials in this volume are still protected by copyright. Prior written permission from Whole Person Press is required if you plan large scale reproduction or distribution of* any portion of this book. If you wish to include any material or adaptation in another publication, you must have permission in writing before proceeding. Please send us your request and proposal at least thirty days in advance.

Structured Exercises are now available in two convenient formats. This small-format softcover version is produced with a new book binding process that stays open on your desk or podium for easy reference, and lies flat on the photocopier for quick duplication of worksheets.

Many trainers enjoy the wide margins and larger type of the full-size looseleaf format, which provides plenty of space for you to add your own workshop designs, examples, chalktalk notes, and process reminders for your presentations. The looseleaf version also includes a complete package of camera-ready worksheet masters for easy reproduction of professional-looking handouts.

☞ See page 152 in the Resources section for complete descriptions and ordering information for worksheet masters and companion volumes of the **Stress** and **Wellness** series in softcover and looseleaf formats.

We are grateful to the many creative trainers who have so generously shared their "best" with you in this volume (see page 146) as well as others in the series. We hope that the ideas here stimulate your own creative juices.

So, go ahead. Strive to bring your teaching alive in new ways. Expand your stress management approach. Continue to touch and motivate people with learning experiences that engage and challenge them as whole persons.

Then let us know what works well for you. We'd love to consider your new ideas for inclusion in a future volume so that we can carry on the tradition of providing this international exchange of innovative teaching designs.

Duluth MN   Nancy Loving Tubesing
January 1994   Donald A Tubesing

vi

INTRODUCTION

Stress is a fact of life—and from the board room to the emergency room to the living room people are searching for ways to manage stress more positively.

Structured Exercises in Stress Management, Volume 2 offers you 36 designs you can use for helping people move beyond information to implementation. Each exercise is structured to creatively involve people in the learning process, whatever the setting and time constraints, whatever the sophistication of the audience. To aid you in the selection of appropriate exercises, they are grouped into six broad categories:

> *Icebreakers:* These short (10–20 minutes) and lively exercises are designed to introduce people to each other and to the subject of stress management. Try combining an icebreaker with an exercise from the assessment or management section for an instant evening program.

> *Stress Assessments:* These exercises explore the symptoms, sources and dynamics of stress. All the processes help people examine the impact of stress in their lives. You'll find a mixture of shorter assessments (30–60 minutes) and major theme developers (60–90 minutes). Any exercise can easily be contracted or expanded to fit your purpose.

> *Management Strategies:* Each of these processes explores the issue of overall strategies for dealing with the stress of life. Participants evaluate their strengths and weaknesses and identify skills for future development.

> *Skill Developers:* Each volume in this handbook series will focus on a few coping skills in more depth. The four exercises in this section highlight relaxation, surrender, laughter and interpersonal contact skills.

> *Action Planning/Closure:* These exercises help participants draw together their insights and determine the actions they wish to take on their own behalf. Some also suggest rituals that bring closure to the group process.

> *Energizers:* The energizers are designed to perk up the group whenever fatigue sets in. Sprinkle them throughout your program to illustrate skills or concepts. Try one for a change of pace—everyone's juices (including yours!) will be flowing again in 5–10 minutes.

The format is designed for easy use. You'll find that each exercise is described completely, including: goals, group size, time frame, materials needed, step-by-step process instructions, and variations.

☞ *Special instructions for the trainer and scripts to be read to the group are typed in italics.*

✔ Questions to ask the group are preceded by a check.

➤ Directions for group activities are indicated by an arrow.

● Mini-lecture notes are preceded by a bullet.

Although the processes are primarily described for large group (25 to 100 people) workshop settings, most of the exercises work just as well with small groups, and many are appropriate for individual therapy or personal reflection.

If you are teaching in the workshop or large group setting, we believe that the use of small discussion groups is the most potent learning structure available to you. We've found that groups of four persons each provide ample air time and a good variety of interaction. If possible, let groups meet together two or three different times during the learning experience before forming new groups.

These personal sharing groups allow people to make positive contact with each other and encourage them to personalize their experience in depth. On evaluations, some people will say "Drop this," others will say, "Give us more small group time," but most will report that the time you give them to share with each other becomes the heart of the workshop.

If you are working with an intact group of 12 people or less, you may want to keep the whole group together for process and discussion time rather than divide into the suggested four or six person groups.

Each trainer has personal strengths, biases, pet concepts and processes. We expect and encourage you to expand and modify what you find here to accommodate your style. Adjust the exercises as you see fit. Bring these designs to life for your participants by inserting your own content and examples into your teaching. Experiment!

And when you come up with something new, let us know . . .

CONTENTS

Preface v

Introduction vii

ICEBREAKERS

37 INTRODUCTIONS 4 1

In these three quick icebreakers, participants introduce themselves with name-matching copers, share their reasons for
attending the course and articulate their stress management
"wishes." (10–20 minutes)

A Alphabet Copers 1
B Personal/Professional 2
C Wave the Magic Wand 2

38 TURTLE, HARE OR RACEHORSE? 5

In this energizing mixer participants take on the identity of the
animal whose life patterns most closely resemble their own.
These "habitat" groups discuss the eustress and distress caused
by their lifestyle. (20–30 minutes)

39 FOUR QUADRANT QUESTIONS 9

In the first segment of this two part exercise participants get
acquainted in small groups as they explore stress management
styles. (15–20 minutes) In the follow-up meeting at the session's
end, group members answer their own questions about
stress. (10–15 minutes)

40 LIFE EVENT BINGO 12

Participants use the Social Readjustment Rating Scale life
events as a bingo card in this get-acquainted exercise.
(10–20 minutes)

41 EXCLUSIVE INTERVIEW 14

Participants pair up for in-depth interviews on stress and coping
skills. (25–30 minutes)

STRESS ASSESSMENTS

42 THE FOURTH SOURCE OF STRESS 17

This exercise points out the role that poor self-esteem plays in creating distress, and helps participants become aware of the power of positive self-esteem as a primary stress management tool. (45–60 minutes)

43 BURNOUT INDEX 25

Using this quick checklist of stress-related symptoms, participants may ascertain their level of stress as well as the likelihood that they will experience burnout. (10–15 minutes)

44 DRAGNET 28

In this stress assessment participants "unravel the mystery" of their stress by recording the facts and analyzing the clues they uncover. (30–40 minutes)

45 BACK TO THE DRAWING BOARD 32

In this major exercise participants analyze the drainers and energizers of their work environment by drawing a symbolic picture of their work setting. (50–75 minutes)

46 LIFETRAP 2: HOOKED ON HELPING 36

Participants affirm the admirable nature of their caring for others and also examine the long-term stress and resulting exhaustion that is inevitable when care-giving becomes an addiction. Although this extended, multi-process exercise is designed for "professional" helpers (nurses, counselors, clergy, teachers, etc), the issues apply to all caring people—especially working parents. (60–90 minutes)

47 CIRCUIT OVERLOAD 46

This assessment tool helps participants to see how much stress they are currently "loading on the circuits."(15–20 minutes)

MANAGEMENT STRATEGIES

48 I'VE GOT RHYTHM **49**

This simple stress management strategy is based on the concept that there's a "right" time for everything. Participants identify the current rhythm of their lives and decide what plans will help them flow with, rather than fight against their natural rhythm. (15–20 minutes)

49 PILEUP COPERS **54**

Using a unique deck of coping cards from the game "PILEUP" participants gain an overall view of possible coping options and identify their personal coping style, by sorting and discussing both the negative and positive coping cards. (60 minutes)

50 MONTH OF FUNDAYS **61**

Participants explore the power of play as a stress management resource and make a plan for incorporating play into their lifestyle every day of the coming month. (20–30 minutes)

51 THE WORRY STOPPER **64**

In this thought-provoking chalktalk and assessment, participants use the criteria of control and importance to determine what's worth worrying about. (30–40 minutes)

52 CONSULTANTS UNLIMITED **70**

Participants act as a consultation team engaged to devise alternative strategies for managing each others' "on-the-job" stressors. (30–40 minutes)

SKILL BUILDERS

53 ATTITUDE ADJUSTMENT HOUR **73**

In this lively exercise participants practice the art of altering their viewpoint by telling and retelling the stories of their day from different perspectives. (25–35 minutes)

54 SPEAK UP! **77**

Participants explore the value of assertiveness as a coping skill by pairing up and experimenting with alternative styles both for making requests and for saying "no." (40–45 minutes)

55 AFFIRMATIVE ACTION PLAN **81**

In this attitude-changing exercise participants draw up a plan for using affirmation to manage a workplace stressor. (40–50 minutes)

56 ANCHORING **88**

Participants guide one another through a relaxation fantasy and "anchor" the comfortable feelings they experience for later recall and stimulation of the relaxation response. (30 minutes)

57 THE ABC'S OF TIME **92**

This skill-building exercise illustrates the importance of spending time where it counts. Participants list the activities and tasks that consumed yesterday's 24 hours, then assess whether or not they invested effort in their top priorities. (40–50 minutes)

PLANNING & CLOSURE

58 PERSONAL/PROFESSIONAL REVIEW **97**

Participants review the session and affirm what they have gained from the learning experience. (10–15 minutes)

59 MANAGER OF THE YEAR **98**

In this closing affirmation participants write recommendations for themselves and campaign for "Stress Manager of the Year" awards. (45–60 minutes)

60 GOALS, OBSTACLES AND ACTIONS **102**

This in-depth planning exercise helps participants set goals, formulate strategies for moving toward their goals, and monitor their progress. (60 minutes)

61 25 WORDS OR LESS **108**

Participants exchange advice for managing stress. (10–15 minutes)

62 STRESS AND COPING JOURNAL **110**

This on-going homework assignment helps participants monitor their stress and apply the management techniques learned during a several week course. (5–10 minutes; three 15–30 minute homework periods)

GROUP ENERGIZERS

63 THE GARDEN **113**

This poignant parable focuses on the difference between "play" and "scoring." (5 minutes)

64 HAND-TO-HAND CONTACT **115**

In this soothing relaxation break participants trade hand massages. (10 minutes)

65 HELPERS ANONYMOUS **118**

In this tongue-in-cheek initiation rite, participants confess their addiction to helping and learning the HA theme song. (5 minutes)

66 MUSICAL MOVEMENT **120**

A montage of musical styles provides the background and beat for tension-reducing interpretive movement. (10–15 minutes)

67 ROUND OF APPLAUSE **122**

In this hand-warming and heart-warming energizer participants applaud their accomplishments and give each other a standing ovation. (2 minutes)

68 SEAWEED AND OAK **123**

Participants alter their energy flow, using fantasy to become as flexible as floating seaweed and as sturdy as an oak tree. (5–10 minutes)

69 STRESS STRETCHERS **125**

Rubberbands illustrate the tension/relaxation dynamics of stress and demonstrate the need for creativity in coping. (5–10 minutes)

70 TARGET PRACTICE **127**

Participants choose a coping skill and experiment with using it during a coffee or lunch break. (10 minutes)

71 TEN-SECOND BREAK **129**

Participants learn a ten-second breathing and auto-suggestion break that's ideal for instant stress relief. (5 minutes)

72 TREASURE CHEST **131**

In this colorful guided fantasy participants discover a treasure chest containing a "gift" they need. (15–20 minutes)

RESOURCES

GUIDE TO THE RESOURCE SECTION **135**

TIPS FOR TRAINERS **136**

EDITOR'S CHOICE **138**

Four****Exercises: The Best of **Stress 2**
Especially for the Workplace

WINNING COMBINATIONS **141**

One-Shot Stress and Coping Presentations
Workshops on Stress and Self-Esteem
Hooked on Helping Workshop for Care-Givers

ANNOTATED INDEXES **143**

Index to Chalktalks
Index to Demonstrations
Index to Physical Energizers
Index to Mental Energizers
Index to Relaxation Routines

CONTRIBUTORS/EDITORS **149**

WHOLE PERSON PUBLICATIONS **153**

Icebreakers

37 INTRODUCTIONS 4

In these three quick icebreakers, participants introduce themselves with name-matching copers (**Alphabet Copers**), share their reasons for attending the course (**Personal/Professional**) and articulate their stress management "wishes" (**Wave the Magic Wand**).

GOALS

To get acquainted.

To heighten awareness of personal goals.

GROUP SIZE

Unlimited; some adjustments may be necessary with very large or very small groups.

TIME FRAME

10–20 minutes

PROCESS

Introduction A: ALPHABET COPERS

1) The trainer invites participants to introduce themselves to the group in a memorable way.

> ➤ Think of a coping technique that could be used to manage stress—one that also begins with the *same first letter* as your first or last name.

> ☞ *You may need to prime the pump with a few examples (eg, "I'm Sally Thomas and my coper is 'Smoking' or 'Talking about it'"). Be sure to include both positive and negative copers in your examples. Allow people a minute or two to think of a good self-introduction.*

2) Participants introduce themselves one by one, stating their names and the matching coper.

> ☞ *With more than 20 people, divide into smaller groups (8–16) for this exercise.*

VARIATION

■ After *Step 2*, the trainer could challenge the group to see how quickly they can learn everyone's name using the companion copers as cues.

Introduction B: PERSONAL/PROFESSIONAL

1) The trainer invites participants to focus on their reasons for coming to the session/workshop, noting that most people sign up for stress management courses with mixed motivations—anticipating they will be able to apply what they learn to their personal life as well as to their job situation.

2) One-by-one participants introduce themselves to others in the group and share their responses to the following sentence stems:

➤ One thing I'm hoping to gain *personally* from this session . . .

➤ One thing I'm hoping to gain *professionally* (or for my job situation) . . .

☞ *If the group is larger than 20 participants, form smaller groups of 3–12 persons for the introductions.*

3) The trainer summarizes the expectations implicit in participants' introductions and highlights the similarity/variety of reasons that motivate participation.

☞ *Personal/Professional Review (p 97) would be especially appropriate as a closing exercise when this process is used as an icebreaker.*

Introduction C: WAVE THE MAGIC WAND

1) The trainer invites participants to imagine they have a fairy godmother who can wave her magic wand and grant any wish they make regarding their life stress or coping style. Each person is to consider his current life situation and decide what stress management "wish" he would like granted.

☞ *You may want to give several examples of stress management "wishes" (eg, "I wish I could stop worrying so much," "I'd like to be able to laugh at myself more," "I wish someone would take off all the pressure," "I need help meeting deadlines," "Get my boss off my back," "Stop all the arguments at home," "Keep my kids out of trouble," etc). The "wishes" do not have to be practical or logical.*

2) Participants introduce themselves to others in the group by stating what "wish" for improving their stress level or coping capacity they would want their fairy godmother to grant them.

☞ *With groups larger than 20, divide participants into smaller units of 6–10 for these introductions.*

VARIATION

■ This process could be used effectively as a feedback and closure exercise at the end of a workshop. Participants would then "wave their magic wands" for one another, telling each group member how they imagine he will manage his stress more positively.

TRAINER'S NOTES

TRAINER'S NOTES

38 TURTLE, HARE OR RACEHORSE?

In this energizing mixer participants take on the identity of the animal whose life patterns most closely resemble their own. These "habitat" groups discuss the eustress and distress caused by their lifestyle.

GOALS

To affirm personal lifestyle patterns.

To identify lifestyle-related eustress and distress.

To promote interaction among participants.

GROUP SIZE

15–40 works best.

TIME FRAME

20–30 minutes; more with larger groups.

MATERIALS

Newsprint posters labeled *Tortoise, Hare* and *Thoroughbred*; markers.

PROCESS

1) The trainer introduces the exercise by noting some or all of the following points:

   ● Over time people develop a lifestyle pattern that works for them. Some folks go at a slow and steady pace, others hop around from crisis to crisis or challenge to challenge. Still others seem to race through life in high gear taking everything in stride.

   ● There is nothing intrinsically right or wrong about any of these lifestyle patterns. Each has its own stresses and strains, joys and rewards.

   ● Hans Selye, one of the pioneer stress researchers, suggests that the key to effective stress management is to find out which pattern fits you—and then live it!

2) The trainer invites participants to consider their own typical life patterns, comparing them to the mythical tortoise, hare and

thoroughbred. As the trainer reads the descriptions, each participant decides which of the animals she resembles most.

- **TORTOISE:**
  Likes to move ahead slowly and steadily.
  Doesn't let others rush her.
  Finds strength from pulling in her head.
  Has a strong protective shell.
  Doesn't take unnecessary risks.
  Prefers life on an even keel without crisis.
  Paces herself, takes one thing at a time.

- **HARE:**
  Moves with quick starts and stops.
  Produces well under pressure.
  Finds strength in exploration and challenge.
  Is fragile, agile and lucky.
  Enjoys risks and adventures.
  Hops from crisis to crisis, is easily distracted.
  Always has many irons in the fire.

- **THOROUGHBRED:**
  Economy and grace of movement.
  Varies pace according to situation.
  Strength comes from top-flight conditioning.
  Always under control.
  Thrives on competition and challenge.
  Has clear goals with mileposts to mark progress along the way.
  Always has something left for the stretch.

3) The trainer designates separate areas of the room as "habitats" for the three animals, using newsprint posters to designate which is which. Participants move to the "habitat" of the animal whose lifestyle description most closely resembles their own.

> 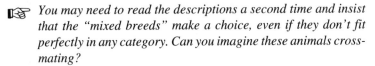 *You may need to read the descriptions a second time and insist that the "mixed breeds" make a choice, even if they don't fit perfectly in any category. Can you imagine these animals cross-mating?*

4) The trainer gives instructions for the introductions.

> ➤ Take turns introducing yourselves by stating *what influenced you to choose this animal group.*

> After everyone in the group is introduced, brainstorm together all the real and potential *positive benefits (eustress)* of your lifestyle—the joys, delights, rewards, etc, of being a tortoise, hare or thoroughbred. List these benefits on the left side of the newsprint. Then on the right side, make a list of all the real and potential negative side effects (distress) of your lifestyle.

5) The trainer reconvenes the total group and asks for comments, insights and observations. If the idea doesn't arise spontaneously, the trainer should remind the group how important it is for each person to respect, rather than resist, her own pattern.

VARIATION

■ For adventuresome people, after *Step 4* the trainer may instruct the three groups to race around the room *as a group* at the pace, and with the "style" of their animal. Allow two minutes for planning, then give the starting signal.

TRAINER'S NOTES

TRAINER'S NOTES

39 FOUR QUADRANT QUESTIONS

In the first segment of this two-part exercise participants get acquainted in small groups as they explore stress management styles. In the follow-up meeting at the session's end, group members answer their own questions about stress.

GOALS

To help participants identify their personal stress management style.

To reinforce the value of mutual responsibility for learning.

To promote interaction and mutual respect among participants.

GROUP SIZE

Unlimited; works well with large groups if the space is adequate.

TIME FRAME

Part A, 15–20 minutes; Part B, 10–15 minutes.

MATERIALS

Blank paper.

PROCESS

A. INTRODUCTIONS (15–20 minutes)

1) The trainer announces that he is going to be asking four questions to be answered briefly in writing. Participants are instructed to divide a blank sheet of paper into four quadrants.

I	II
III	IV

2) In *Quadrant I* the trainer asks participants to respond to the following questions:

➤ Think of *a person you know who manages stress extremely well.* Write down that person's name.

➤ What qualities (skills, attitudes, behaviors) make this person such a good stress manager?

3) The trainer invites people to think about their own style of managing stress. In *Quadrant II* participants reply to the question:
   - ➤ Describe your personal stress management style. What are your strong/weak coping skills? How do you tackle stressful situations?

4) The trainer directs participants to review their day so far, and in *Quadrant III* to answer one of the following questions:
   - ➤ In what ways did you experience stress in coming to this session today? *OR*
   - ➤ How have you experienced stress so far in this session?

5) In *Quadrant IV*, participants respond to the inquiry:
   - ➤ What's one question you have about stress?

6) The trainer directs participants to find a partner. Once everyone is paired off, partners share their answers from *Quadrant III*—how they experienced stress today. (2–3 minutes)

7) The trainer asks each duo to join with another pair to make a foursome, and gives instructions for small group discussion.
   - ➤ Take turns sharing your responses from *Quadrants I* and *II*. The person whose first name comes first in the alphabet should begin.
   - ➤ Elaborate your answer as much as you want. Whenever you run out of steam, pass the spotlight to the next person in the alphabet.
   - ➤ When everyone is finished, spend the remaining time comparing, contrasting and expanding your insights.
   - ➤ You will have a total of 10 minutes for sharing.

8) The trainer reconvenes the group and comments that this exercise has offered an opportunity for participants to clarify their own thinking and expand each others' understanding of stress. He indicates that discussion of the questions in the fourth quadrant will be saved until later in the session. The trainer proceeds with the major content portion of the course.

B. REVIEW (10–15 minutes)

9) At some point near the end of the session (or course), after participants have received the essential content on stress and stress management, the trainer instructs people to rejoin the small groups established for the first part of this exercise.

One-by-one, participants ask the questions they had written in **Quadrant IV**. The group discusses possible answers to each question, based on what they have learned during the session.

10) The trainer reconvenes the large group and asks for examples of questions and answers generated by the small groups. He uses these as a springboard for expanding, clarifying and summarizing the session content.

TRAINER'S NOTES

We first learned this process from Joel Goodman.

40 LIFE EVENT BINGO

Participants use the Social Readjustment Rating Scale life events as a bingo card in this get-acquainted exercise.

GOALS

To discover the diversity of coping techniques people use in dealing with stressful life events.

To introduce the group and the topic in an entertaining manner.

GROUP SIZE

Best with groups of 15–20 or more persons.

TIME FRAME

10–30 minutes

MATERIALS

Life Event Bingo worksheet for all participants.

PROCESS

1) The trainer distributes the **Life Event Bingo** sheets, and gives instructions for the mixer.

   ➤ Move around in the group, introducing yourself and searching for individuals who have experienced each life event *within the past year.* When you find someone who has experienced a particular event, interview him to find out what coping technique was most useful in dealing with that change. Write the person's name and most effective copers in the appropriate space and move on to meet a new person who coped with a different life change in the past year.

   🖙 *Depending on the time available, play "5-in-a-row" or "full-card" Bingo. Remind participants that their emphasis should be on making contact with others in the group and learning about the variety of coping skills people use in response to stressful situations. Filling the Bingo card is only a secondary goal.*

2) The trainer reconvenes the group and asks what they learned about stress, change, coping and each other.

LIFE EVENT BINGO

Find someone here who has experienced these life events during the past year. Introduce yourself and ask that person to describe the coping technique that worked best for them in that situation and write the coper in the appropriate box. Try to find a different person for each event.

divorce	death of spouse	jail term	marriage	change in work responsibilities
change in financial status	son or daughter leaves home	business readjustment	starting or stopping school	added someone to the family
change in personal habits	retirement	outstanding personal achievement	death of a close friend	more arguments with spouse
pregnancy	change in residence	change in working hours/conditions	personal illness or injury	death of a close family member
change to different line of work	trouble with the in-laws	sickness in family	fired from job	took out a mortgage

41 EXCLUSIVE INTERVIEW

Participants get acquainted by pairing up for in-depth interviews on stress and coping skills.

GOALS

To explore personal stress management styles.

To provide an initial bonding experience that models personal sharing and peer support.

GROUP SIZE

Unlimited.

TIME FRAME

25–30 minutes; could be shortened with some loss of depth.

MATERIALS

Leading Questions handout for everyone.

PROCESS

1) The trainer distributes the **Leading Questions** handout and announces that everyone is going to have an opportunity to play the role of *cub reporter* interviewing a local *celebrity*.

2) Participants are asked to choose a partner (preferably someone they don't know well) and move to a relatively private space in the room. Each pair decides who will be the celebrity and who will be the *reporter* in the first round.

3) The trainer gives instructions for the interview.

   ➤ *Reporters* should spend the next 10 minutes pursuing an in-depth interview of your *celebrity* partner, using whatever leading questions from the handout seem appropriate. The goal of the interview is to learn as much as possible about the *celebrity's* stress patterns and coping style.

   ➤ *Celebrities* should answer the questions as completely as you feel comfortable, keeping in mind the goal of getting a new perspective on your own stress management patterns.

4) After 10 minutes, the trainer asks all **Reporters** to write down a "lead sentence" for their article about the *Celebrity* they interviewed.

> ☞ *You may want to give some examples, such as, "Moving has never bothered Tom Marcus — he's an expert at instant relationships." Or "Susan Antwerp's favorite coping technique is an oatmeal facial." Or "Quit hoping... start coping. That's Amelia Winter's advice for the stressed." Remind reporters to use the celebrity's name in the sentence.*

5) *Reporters* and *Celebrities* switch roles for the second 10-minute interview. At the end of the interview, the **Reporter** writes a lead sentence.

6) The trainer suggests that partners briefly discuss their reactions to the process and what they learned about themselves.

7) The trainer reconvenes the whole group and asks participants to introduce their partners by reading their lead sentences.

VARIATIONS

■ The trainer could conduct group interviews with 6–8 persons at a time. The group to be interviewed forms a circle at the front. The remaining participants observe while the trainer facilitates the small group's discussion of one or more leading questions. Several groups could be interviewed in this *fishbowl* fashion, each answering different questions. The trainer may invite onlookers to comment or ask additional questions.

■ Instead of pairing up for interviews, participants could divide into small groups (4–8 people) for discussion of one or more leading questions assigned by the trainer.

■ This exercise could be expanded into a theme-building chalktalk by asking each participant to choose one question from the list and respond to it in writing. The trainer collects the paragraphs, reads them out loud and elaborates on the issues and concerns raised in the answers.

LEADING QUESTIONS

How would you define stress?

When do you feel most stressed?

Where in your body do you feel stress?

What people in your life cause you stress?

How do you feel before, during and after a stressful situation?

What situations do you "breeze through" that seem stressful
   to others?

In what ways is stress "good" for you?

What are some of the special stressors that go along with
   different
   life stages?

What coping skills have you found the most helpful in dealing
   with stress?

What situation is extremely stressful to you, but doesn't seem to
   bother other people?

What is the key ingredient in stress management?

What advice would you give someone about the best way to
   manage stress?

What's the most stressful life experience you can imagine? Why
   would it be so stressful?

What has been the most stressful period in your life so far?
   What skills did you use to deal with it?

How do/did your parents deal with stress?

What's the biggest source of stress for you at work?

Stress
Assessments

42 FOURTH SOURCE OF STRESS

This exercise points out the role that poor self-esteem plays in creating distress, and helps participants become aware of the power of positive self-esteem as a primary stress management tool.

GOALS

To acknowledge poor self-esteem as the primary and most common sources of distress.

To understand the importance of positive self-esteem in the management of day-to-day stress.

To help participants assess and improve their opinion of themselves.

GROUP SIZE

Unlimited.

TIME FRAME

45–60 minutes

MATERIALS

Self-Esteem Checklist and **Messages From My Past** worksheets for each participant.

PROCESS

☞ *This exercise is divided into five sequential segments which could be used independently or in some other combination. Life Event Bingo (p 12) would fit well as a warm-up.*

   A) The Sources of Stress—chalktalk (15–20 minutes)
   B) Self-Esteem as the Key—chalktalk (5–10 minutes)
   C) Assessing Self-Esteem—checklist (10–15 minutes)
   D) Origins of Self-Esteem—worksheet (10–15 minutes)
   E) Improving Self-Esteem—suggestions (5–10 minutes)

A. The Sources of Stress (15–20 minutes)

1) The trainer outlines the *four major sources of stress* according to the following model.

- **Customary, anticipated life events.** These events represent the transitions of normal life (eg, graduating from high school or college, marriage, having children, moving to a new home, changing jobs, retiring, etc).

  They can be influenced, but not totally controlled, by personal decisions. Normally, they cause a positive, stimulating form of stress. Symptoms of distress may be experienced when several of these events cluster in a short time period or when we resist the changes represented by the events.

- **Unexpected life events**. These events are the "tragedies" and "shocks" of life (eg, being involved in an accident, being the victim of a crime, the sudden death of a loved one, losing one's job, etc).

  These stressors usually occur to us suddenly, without warning, and are not in our control. The stress symptoms that result are also often sudden, and sometimes severe. Normally, however, such symptoms do not become chronic. With time we heal and the symptoms are relieved.

- **Progressive accumulating events**. These represent the everyday strains of life, especially unresolved stressors in close relationships (eg, ongoing conflict with spouse, continuing parent-child friction, long-term care for a disabled relative, boredom with a career path, cumulative job-related pressures, etc).

  The symptoms of stress-exhaustion resulting from these factors develop slowly, but because they accumulate over time, they are not easily dissipated. The magnitude of these pressures often seem to gain momentum, as the "victims" feel increasingly worn out and unable to cope.

- **Personal trait stress**. This self-imposed stress caused by perfectionism, insecurity, lack of self confidence, feelings of jealousy or inadequacy, is the only source of stress over which we have total control.

  Stress caused by low self-esteem pervades all daily situations and influences all interactions. Sufferers often become anxious worriers, plagued by generalized feelings of fear and disease. These symptoms are often chronic and life-long unless the source of the stress—negative feelings about self—is changed.

2) The trainer may ask participants, individually or as a group, to identify their predominant sources of stress based on this paradigm. A discussion of their findings may follow.

B. Self-Esteem as the Key (5–10 minutes)

3) The trainer outlines the role of self-esteem by sharing the following thoughts:

- **Love your neighbor as yourself** is a saying familiar to most of us. It means that you must have the capacity to love and accept yourself in order to form and keep satisfying relationships with others. Self-esteem means accepting yourself for who you really are and believing that you are indeed a worth-while person who is deserving of love and respect from others.

- **Self-esteem is your sense of how good you feel about yourself.** It is based on your judgment of yourself, not on other people's assessment. Your self-esteem does not depend on your talent. Some very ordinary people feel very good about themselves, while other *extra*-ordinary high achievers hold low opinions of themselves.

- **Self-esteem is the primary key to long-term stress management.** Why? The first three sources of stress (predictable life events, unexpected changes and the build-up of daily strains) are much easier to handle when we believe in ourselves. A positive, healthy self-esteem gives us the "hardiness to roll with the punches" of life, and to see them as challenges to be met, rather than threats to be feared.

- **The fourth category of stressors, personal patterns, is entirely the result of a low self-esteem.** It's this category of stress that is most pervasive and exhausting over the long run. Personal trait stress cannot be overcome, or even altered, until the self-esteem problems that cause it are corrected.

4) The trainer solicits from the group examples of people they know (including themselves) whose self-esteem has contributed to their stress or limited their coping capabilities. She then asks for illustrations of people whose healthy self-esteem has had a positive impact on their stress management capacity.

C. Assessing Self-Esteem (10–15 minutes)

5) The trainer instructs participants to complete the **Self-Esteem Checklist** by marking their response to each of the fourteen questions.

6) Participants pair up with a partner. The trainer then asks participants to share their responses to the following questions.

©1994 Whole Person Press 210 W Michigan Duluth MN 55802   (800) 247-6789

➤ In what ways does your self-esteem make you more vulnerable to stress?

➤ In what ways does your self-esteem contribute to your "hardiness" and your ability to deal with life's stressors?

➤ How do you feel about your current level of self-esteem?

➤ How might you increase your "hardiness" by improving your self-esteem?

D. The Origins of Self-Esteem (10–15 minutes)

7) The trainer points out to participants that the first step in improving their image of themselves is to gain an awareness of the roots of their current self-esteem. Participants then complete the **Messages From My Past** worksheet. (5 minutes)

8) Partners share their answers and discuss any insights that occur to them. (5 minutes)

☞ *You might also ask participants to compare their responses to the following questions:*

What patterns or themes do you notice in your messages from the past?

Are these messages accurate descriptions of you today?

Which need revision? Which could/should be discarded? Which do you cherish?

9) The trainer challenges the group by observing:

● "What we *are* may be our parents' fault, what we *remain* is our responsibility!"

● "Be sure you are not handicapping yourself with low self-esteem, just because of someone's ill-timed remark years ago."

E. Improving Self-Esteem (5–10 minutes)

10) The trainer may offer some or all of the following suggestions for taking the first steps toward improving personal self-esteem.

● **Speak up for yourself**. Your opinion is valid. No one can "put you down" unless you "put them up" by deciding their viewpoint is worth more than yours. Resist such belittling thoughts.

- **Don't put yourself down**. Nobody's perfect. Mistakes and failures are a normal component of life—welcome to the human race! Instead of criticizing yourself, forgive yourself.
- **Remember—you're in charge of your life**. Think for yourself! Make your own decisions! Trust your process!
- **Get off the pity pot**. Don't indulge in guilt trips or blaming and shaming routines.
- **Believe in yourself**. Stop counting on others to tell you that you count. Tell yourself!
- **Be all that you can be**. Don't depend on others to do things for you that you are capable of doing for yourself—even if they could do a better job!
- **Tend to your needs**. Don't neglect yourself or subvert your needs in order to meet the needs of others.
- **Be proud of yourself**. You are unique and your very existence proves your innate worth. Don't forget it!

11) The trainer concludes the exercise by inviting participants to describe whatever insights have occurred to them during the process. Participants may also share any personal resolutions for improving their self-esteem.

VARIATION

■ This exercise could be expanded to include an in-depth exploration of all four sources of stress. As part of *Step 1* the trainer presents additional information on life events stress, using the Holmes and Rahe *Social Readjustment Rating Scale* as an assessment tool. Participants complete the scale for themselves, then decide as a group which items fall in the "anticipated" category and which in the "unexpected" category. The trainer solicits examples of the third source of stress— accumulated unresolved stressors and strain—before moving on to highlight personal trait stress.

Submitted by Gloria Singer.

*The Four Sources of Stress model (Step 1) is summarized from an article by Barbara Brown (A Conceptual Analysis of 'The Stress of Life Phenomenon.' **Stress 2**, 1981). **The Self-Esteem Checklist** is based on a column by Sydney J Harris. The suggestions for improving self-esteem (Step 10) are adapted from Dunlap & Stewart, **Keeping the Fire Alive**, (Tulsa: Penwell Books, 1983).*

SELF-ESTEEM CHECKLIST

AA = ALMOST ALWAYS
O = OCCASIONALLLY
R = RARELY
N= NEVER

1) Do you find yourself bragging or exaggerating the importance of your role?	AA	O	R	N
2) Are you jealous of the possessions, opportunities or positions of others?	AA	O	R	N
3) Do you find yourself judging your behavior by other people's standards or expectations rather than your own?	AA	O	R	N
4) Are you possessive in your relationships with friends and/or family members?	AA	O	R	N
5) Is it difficult for you to acknowledge your own mistakes?	AA	O	R	N
6) Do you resort to bullying and intimidation in your dealings with others?	AA	O	R	N
7) Do you "put people down" so that you can feel "one up"?	AA	O	R	N
8) Are you a perfectionist?	AA	O	R	N
9) Must you be a "winner" in recreational activities in order to have fun?	AA	O	R	N
10) When faced with new opportunities do you feel inadequate or insecure?	AA	O	R	N
11) Do you have difficulty accepting compliments?	AA	O	R	N
12) Do you refrain from expressing your feelings and opinions?	AA	O	R	N
13) Do you shy away from trying new things for fear of failure or looking dumb?	AA	O	R	N
14) Do you neglect your own needs in order to respond to the needs of others?	AA	O	R	N

"ALMOST ALWAYS" or "OFTEN" answers to any of these questions may indicate that your level of self-esteem needs attention.

MESSAGES FROM MY PAST

The messages we have received from people who have been important in our lives contribute to our level of self-esteem. These messages can be positive or negative. In the space below, write the messages you recall receiving from people who have been important to you.

EXAMPLES

Mother—*"You're so rattle-brained! You'd lose your head if it weren't attached to the rest of you!"*

Father—*"That's my daughter—she can do just about anything she sets her mind to."*

Teacher—*"He's not the brightest kid, but he sure tries hard."*

Others—*"How are you going to get ahead if your head is always in the clouds?"*

MY MESSAGES FROM

MOTHER:

FATHER:

SIBLINGS:

CLERGY:

FRIENDS:

TEACHERS:

COACH:

OTHERS:

©1994 Whole Person Press 210 W Michigan Duluth MN 55802   (800) 247-6789

TRAINER'S NOTES

43 BURNOUT INDEX

Using this quick checklist of stress-related symptoms, participants may ascertain their level of stress as well as the likelihood that they will experience burnout.

GOALS

To assess participants' current level of stress.

To indicate that the toll of stress exhaustion is exacted on the whole person, not just the body.

GROUP SIZE

Unlimited; also appropriate for work with individuals.

TIME FRAME

10–15 minutes

MATERIALS

Six Typical Symptoms of Burnout worksheet for each participant.

PROCESS

1) The trainer introduces the concept that a build-up of stress and strain can lead to burnout. He points out that no one is immune to stress exhaustion, covering some or all of the following points:

- Don't be surprised when you see the signs of stress fatigue in yourself and others—because you will. **Many people feel under stress a good share of the time**.

- In an informal survey a remarkable percentage of people in different professions reported that they are usually or always under stress:
  - ○ 80% of executives and managers
  - ○ 66% of teachers and secretaries
  - ○ 67% of farmers
  - ○ 61% of homemakers

- Most burnout symptoms are generalized—that is, they cannot be traced to one particular stressor. **Stress symptoms are signs of overall exhaustion**. Often, therefore, they "just don't make sense" when we try to understand which of our "problems" has caused them.

- **All of us need to be on guard to prevent burnout.** When the symptoms pop up, don't ignore them—take creative action to nip the problem in the bud.

2) Participants complete the **Six Typical Symptoms of Burnout** worksheet. (5 minutes)

3) The trainer outlines the *Burnout Index* scoring code for the test.

   BURNOUT INDEX—a quick rule of thumb:

   A person is close to burnout when they're experiencing TWO of these symptoms,

   has a severe case with FOUR,

   and is terminally ill if all SIX are present!

   If you never recognize any of these symptoms in yourself, ever, you're probably too far gone for help!

4) The trainer may invite a sharing of observations and insights from the group.

TRAINER'S NOTES

Submitted by Thomas G Boman.

©1994 Whole Person Press 210 W Michigan Duluth MN 55802   (800) 247-6789

SIX TYPICAL SYMPTOMS OF BURNOUT

Have you experienced any stress exhaustion symptoms lately?
Make specific notes on symptoms that are regularly part of your life.

1) Irritability and a general distrust of others' intentions.	Y	N
2) No new ideas in the past six months.	Y	N
3) Lack of energy physical and/or emotional.	Y	N
4) Feelings of isolation and lack of personal support.	Y	N
5) Urge to get out of my present job situation.	Y	N
6) An attempt to feel good about myself by focusing on "how much" I do.	Y	N

How many symptoms are you currently experiencing?

What symptoms, other than those listed, are you experiencing?

Which symptoms concern you the most? (in your own words)

"I am particularly concerned when I begin to feel . . ."

Which symptoms would you say are sure signs that if you don't change something you're headed for big trouble?

Any other observations or comments?

44 DRAGNET

In this stress assessment participants "unravel the mystery" of their stress by recording the facts and analyzing the clues they uncover.

GOALS

To identify current stressors.

To analyze the situational circumstances of stressors and to discover the common patterns that connect them.

GROUP SIZE

Unlimited; also effective for work with individuals.

TIME FRAME

30–40 minutes

MATERIALS

Dragnet Stress Analysis and **Suspicions** worksheets for each participant.

PROCESS

1) The trainer distributes both of the worksheets and leads participants through the **Dragnet Stress Analysis.**

   ☞ *Pause long enough between each step to allow the majority of participants to think of several answers.*

   ➤ Make a list of your current stressors in the left-hand column.

   ➤ Now "gather the facts" about your stress. Answer the *What? When? Where? Who? How? Why?* questions for each stressor you have listed.

   ➤ We're interested in "the facts" only, not long essays. The space for writing is intentionally small, but do jot down one or two words in each and every box.

   ☞ *Participants will probably find that in some columns their answers quickly become repetitious. This is appropriate, and will lead to clues for unraveling the mystery of their current stress dilemma.*

2) When most people have filled the worksheet boxes, the trainer inter-
rupts and invites participants to summarize their insights.

➤ Review your notes in *each vertical column* and summarize your
findings about the who's, what's and where's, using the space
provided *at the bottom of the chart*.

➤ Now that you have the "facts" about your stress, stop and take a look
at the overall pattern. Use the **Suspicions** worksheet to analyze the
facts of your stress. List your *suspicions* about your stress and the
areas of promise *for further investigation*.

3) The trainer divides participants into groups of four persons each and
instructs them to share with each other a summary of the "facts of their
case" as well as their list of suspicions and areas for further investigation. (3–4 minutes each, 15–20 minutes overall)

4) The trainer reconvenes the entire group and invites comments on the
themes and insights observed by the group.

TRAINER'S NOTES

DRAGNET STRESS ANALYSIS

Gather the "facts"	The situation? Precipitating actions or interactions? Result/Resolution?	Date? Time of day? How often? Following what? Preceding what?	Location? Work, home, play? Other significant circumstances?	Spouse? Children? Friends? Supervisors? Subordinates? Strangers?	The trigger? The power and force behind it?	Bad attitude? Dirty politics? Stupidity? Circumstances beyond control?
STRESSORS (list 5–8)	**WHAT?**	**WHEN?**	**WHERE?**	**WHO?**	**HOW?**	**WHY?**
Summarize the essential ingredient of each column.						

©1994 Whole Person Press 210 W Michigan Duluth MN 55802   (800) 247-6789

SUSPICIONS

Looking at the clues in this fact-gathering document, the following hunches about my stress mysteries should be investigated further . . . .

I suspect that . . . .

I suspect that . . . .

I suspect that . . . .

FOR FURTHER INVESTIGATION

To unravel the mystery of my current stress, I need to investigate the following options:

I should investigate . . . .

I should investigate . . . .

I should investigate . . . .

45 BACK TO THE DRAWING BOARD

In this major exercise participants analyze the drainers and energizers of their work environment by drawing a symbolic picture of their work setting.

GOALS

To recognize factors in the job setting which produce distress.

To isolate factors in the job setting which nurture and reward.

To identify strategies for coping with organizational, work-related stress.

GROUP SIZE

Unlimited.

TIME FRAME

50–75 minutes

MATERIALS

Blank paper.

PROCESS

1) The trainer distributes blank paper and invites participants to warm-up to the exercise by putting their job in context. (5 minutes)

   ➤ Write a 20–30 word description of the organization in which you work and your specific job. Leave out all subjective value judgments and cynical comments. The descriptions are to be as objective as possible.

   ☞ *Give two or three examples appropriate to your audience (eg, "I am an RN in charge of labor and delivery at a 500-bed hospital that is currently adding two new wings and three new units," or "I am in charge of the midwest region, 18-person sales force for a California-based company specializing in designing computer software packages for small businesses").*

2) The trainer invites 6–10 volunteers to read their objective paragraphs. The remaining participants listen carefully and note the subtle differences in each description.

Even when participants are from the same company the varia-tions in their descriptions are always interesting, sometimes humorous.

Acknowledge the fact that objective definitions are difficult to write when you're so close to, and caught up in, your work.

3) The trainer distributes blank paper and gives instructions for the next step. (10 minutes)

➤ Draw a picture of your organization with yourself in it.

 Assure participants that they need not be artists. They may use symbols, diagrams, words, organizational charts or charac-terizations of key people—to depict the power issues, alle-giances and relationships that exist. Encourage them to get started by drawing the first image that comes to their minds and to then follow their intuitions as they embellish the picture.

4) The trainer asks participants to examine their picture and reflect on their stressors on the job. (5 minutes)

➤ Every job and every work situation has its particular stress—from tasks to relationships to equipment to atmosphere.

➤ Look over your picture and note those factors in your work situation that are the **disturbing, frustrating stress-producers**. Mark these stressors with an *exclamation point (!)*. You may also wish to add a word or two of explanation at these points.

 Choose some or all of the following questions and encourage participants to incorporate their responses into the picture with words, symbols or drawings.

➤ **What's stressful about your work relationships?** with peers, subor-dinates, supervisors, top management, customers; the conflicts, lack of guidance, competition, jealousy, negativism, cynicism?

➤ **What's stressful about the way the organization works?** the pressure, the pace, the way decisions are made, the flow of informa-tion, who gets ahead and how, the hidden agendas, the "rules," the red tape, the reporting requirements, the job descriptions, the busi-ness philosophy?

➤ **What's stressful about the reward system?** the pay, the fringes, the appreciation and affirmation, the budget cuts, the "perks," the parties?

➤ **What's stressful about the physical environment?** the noise level, the equipment, the space?

➤ **What's stressful about the way you fit in and the work you do?**
the tasks, the opportunity for growth or advancement, the skills
required, the deadlines, the quotas, the number of "hats?"

5) The trainer invites participants to shift their focus to the anti-stress
qualities of their work environment.

➤ Every job and every organization also includes "pluses"—the positive, pleasant factors that energize us and draw us back.

➤ Examine your picture again and note these *supportive, nurturing
factors*. Mark these energizers with a *star (*)*. Add a word or two of
explanation at these points if you wish.

6) The trainer solicits from the group 25–30 specific examples of organizational nutrients they included in their drawings. Participants embellish
their drawings with additional relevant energizers as they are suggested.

☞ *If the group gets stuck, highlight several positive factors that may
be present in the workplace:*

> *Gratitude and thanks—from peers, supervisors, subordi-
nates, customers.*

> *Success in completing tasks, clarity in jobs and responsi-
bilities.*

> *Respect, being listened to, power to make decisions.*

> *Common purposes, rituals and traditions.*

> *Good pay, fringes, flexible hours, day care, car pool.*

> *Stimulation, challenge, new ideas, variety.*

> *Comfort, windows, music, beautiful grounds.*

> *Adequate staff, assistance, budget.*

> *Friendship, support, positive people, harmonious rela-
tionships.*

7) The trainer divides the participants into small groups (4–6 persons), for
discussion. (20–30 minutes)

➤ Take 4–5 minutes each to show your picture to your group and
summarize its meaning. Share your assessment of the stressors and
the energizers in your current work environment.

☞ *If participants are from the same work setting, they should be
encouraged to share only as much as they feel is comfortable
and prudent.*

8) The trainer reconvenes the group and asks participants to help him
construct a list of *Principles for Surviving in the Work World* that can

be gleaned from this exercise. The trainer records the major points on the blackboard/overhead as they emerge.

Issues that may be highlighted by the trainer if they are not volunteered by the group include:

- **Take the bad with the good**—every job has its rewards as well as its trials.

- **Analyze your work setting**—not only from an efficiency point of view, but also in light of the energizers available for refueling.

- **Set up a mutual admiration society**—everyone needs to be appreciated. If one person won't do it, find someone else. Compliment each other.

- **Know what you can and what you cannot change**—some battles are worth fighting, others are not.

- **Avoid all unnecessary meetings**—the number of meetings and the likelihood of burnout are positively correlated.

- **Be a good bureaucrat**—the ability to influence is the key to power. Play your cards wisely. Learn how to make a positive difference in the setting with whatever power you can muster.

- **Experiment with revitalization**—no one strategy for surviving will work all the time. Be adventurous. Try something new for fun. Surprise someone!

VARIATION

■ The length of this exercise can be shortened by dropping the embellishment process in *Steps 4–5*. Participants will still have great energy for, and find meaning in, sharing their symbolic pictures with each other.

46 LIFETRAP 2: HOOKED ON HELPING

Participants affirm the admirable nature of their caring for others and also examine the long-term stress and resulting exhaustion that is inevitable when care-giving becomes an addiction. Although this extended, multi-process exercise is designed for "professional" helpers (nurses, counselors, clergy, teachers, etc), the issues apply to all caring people—especially working parents.

GOALS

To recognize, affirm and rejoice in care-giving commitments.

To examine the stress that results when people get hooked on caring for others first, regardless of the cost to self.

To explore options for controlling the care-giver's addiction while still reaching out in caring commitments to others.

GROUP SIZE

Unlimited.

TIME FRAME

60–90 minutes

MATERIALS

Blank paper; one copy of the **Hooked on Helping Addiction Test** and **Hooked on Helping Beliefs** worksheets for each participant.

PROCESS

☞ *This is a five-part exercise:*
   A) Introductory chalktalk on the care-giving addiction.
   (5–10 minutes)
   B) Guided reflection process exploring personal care-giving qualities. (15–20 minutes)
   C) Personal assessment using the Hooked on Helping Addiction Test and the Hooked on Helping Beliefs Inventory. (15–20 minutes)
   D) Small group sharing. (20–30 minutes)
   E) Wrap-up with strategies for coping. (5–10 minutes)

A. Care-Giving: A Stress-Producing Lifetrap (5–10 minutes)

1) The trainer introduces the subject of care-giving by soliciting from the group examples of the "helpful" things participants have done that day (eg, made lunch for my daughter, took the dog for a walk, drove a colleague to work, gave Mr James a backrub, bit back an angry retort, paid attention to my spouse, took an emergency call, cleaned up the bathroom, earned money for house payment, juggled work assignments, etc).

    ☞ *If the group is not composed of "professional" care-givers who identify immediately with the issues raised here, you may want to provide a more extensive warm-up to the topic. Ask "How many people here did something helpful today?" Solicit lots of examples. Then ask, "How many of you enjoy the process of doing something nice or caring for someone else?" Invite participants to describe how they feel when they've been helpful.*

2) After the group has generated a wide variety of helping behaviors, the trainer points out that all of us are care-givers—sensitive, lively people who reach out to others and touch them. Unfortunately, this lifestyle can become a seductive lifetrap that breeds stress. The trainer outlines the *Hooked on Helping* addiction process:

    ● **We care-givers are admirable people**. We usually have our antennae turned outwards toward others and whenever we pick up signals of need, we are prompted to respond, to reach out.

    ● **Care-giving is extremely fulfilling**. It's rewarding to be sensitive, warm, loving and involved in others' lives. It also feels wonderful to be recognized as a special, caring, loving person.

    ● **In fact, helping feels so satisfying that it's possible to get hooked on the experience**, becoming addicted to the payoffs of putting others' needs first. The admirable quality of caring for others also bears the risk of shortchanging ourselves.

    ● Hooked helpers know how to turn their compassion faucet "on" so their love flows out, but have forgotten how to turn the faucet "off." **Addicted care-givers are particularly vulnerable to stress exhaustion**. When helpers spend months and even years caring for a parade of "others" without also caring for themselves, they may burn out—and end up feeling empty and bitter.

    ● How do people get hooked on helping? We get hooked by our beliefs and life experience, starting at an early age. Many helpers come from families where caring for others was rewarded and "selfishness" was discouraged. Even though fulfilling all the family's wishes and demands would be impossible, "helper" children believe that they have the responsibility to take care of everyone else, regardless of their own feelings. **Our beliefs keep us hooked on helping well into adulthood.**

B. Examining the Care-Giver in You (15–20 minutes)

3) The trainer distributes blank paper and invites participants to get in touch with the wonderful, warm, gentle spirit of care-giving in themselves by reflecting on the following questions.

☞ *This series of questions works best when participants do not know the sequence ahead of time. Ask the questions one at a time, allowing ample opportunity for participants to answer each one thoughtfully before moving on.*

➤ Think of *a person whom you would consider a model of caring and helpfulness*—a helpful hero or heroine, if you will. This person may be dead or alive, known to you personally or only by reputation. Write down this person's name at the top of your page.

➢ In your mind consider this person. What is she like? How is she helpful? What are her *qualities of caring* that you admire most? Write them down.

➢ *How are you like that person?* Or in what ways would you like to emulate that person? Make note of these similarities and desired qualities.

➤ Think back to your earliest memories and make a note of *the first time you can recall being "helpful."* Perhaps it was when you washed the dishes for your mother, or defended a sibling, or assisted your first grade teacher. Jot down a few details about your first recollection of being "helpful."

➢ As you consider that early occasion, what were the *qualities of helpfulness that you demonstrated* in that instance? (eg, did work, gave encouragement, came to someone's defense, listened carefully, etc).

➤ Think about yourself as a caring, helpful person. *When you're at your very best—what is it that you give to others?*

©1994 Whole Person Press 210 W Michigan Duluth MN 55802   (800) 247-6789

➤ Think back to the time when you started your present profession (job/role/etc). *What grand visions of caring and helping did you carry into your job when you started?* (These dreams and visions may be very tender—the kind of sensitive issues you usually don't talk about.) Write these visions down with all the excitement and grandiosity that you can recall feeling when you were fresh and idealistic.

● The ultimate helper's fantasy goes something like this:
   "I can: (a) work a miracle . . . (b) in a hopeless situation . . . (c) because I care so much."

● Few people ever really say this out loud, but most care-givers recognize the fantasy. There are countless variations, such as:
   ○ Helping someone whom no one else could help—by giving time or love . . .
   ○ Single-handedly changing a bureaucratic system and being appreciated for it . . .
   ○ Hoping you could take away someone's pain, by caring so much . . .

➤ Write some *detailed notes on your fantasy* about how you can (a) work a miracle, (b) in a hopeless situation, (c) because you care so much.

➤ Look over all your answers and notice the rich variety of caring characteristics you've identified. Then *write a paragraph describing yourself as if you possess every single caring quality you've identified* (including those of your helpful hero/heroine).

Don't hedge by saying you're only this way some of the time. Write the paragraph as if you are all of these fine qualities all of the time. For example, you might write:
   I am sensitive, and when others are hurting I always listen and give them all the time that they need. I am loyal and trustworthy. People can depend on me to come through when they need me . . . etc . . . etc . . .

4) When participants have completed their paragraphs, the trainer asks them to form groups of four persons each. The trainer gives instructions.

➤ Get acquainted by reading your paragraphs out loud to each other.

➤ Brag wholeheartedly, introducing yourself by describing all your helpful qualities in full detail.

☞ *Participants will groan when you give this assignment. Don't worry. Simply laugh and tell them, "If you think God will get you for doing this, tell God—'the trainer up front made me do it!'" Instruct participants to refrain from any side comments that would undercut their bragging (eg, "Well, I'm not that way all the time, and sometimes I'm also crabby," etc). Participants are to brag only, and feel how it feels!*

5) The trainer reconvenes the group and asks for reactions. Undoubtedly, reactions will be mixed—"It was silly." "It felt good." "It was embarrassing." The trainer may point out the following concepts.

● Most people are "closet braggers"—they want others to notice these good qualities but don't want others to notice that they're trying to get them to notice!

● The tender visions of caring and kindness we all carry in our hearts are powerful, positive motivators, not to be denied or diminished, but to be relished and enjoyed!

● In one sense, **stress exhaustion is a compliment!** It "attacks" only those who care—those who sparkle with enthusiasm for life. You have to have been *on fire* to burn out. Those who glow with enthusiasm for people are the ones who experience the symptoms of burnout from caring—too much!

C. Exploring the Trap of Addiction (15–20 minutes)

6) In order to help participants assess their own level of addiction to care-giving, the trainer distributes **Hooked on Helping Addiction Tests** to the group members and asks them to answer every question "yes" or "no," as honestly as they can.

7) Participants total their "yes" responses and judge their addiction level according to the following scale as read by the trainer.

> *0–1 = NOT ADDICTED: People in this category may very well be excellent care-givers—but they have also learned how to include themselves on their care list!*

> *2–4 = BORDERLINE ADDICTION: The process of care-giving will at times exhaust these folks to the point where they feel they "have no more to give." They will probably experience resulting symptoms of distress.*

5–7 = ADDICTED CARE-GIVERS: The unrestrained attempt to care for everyone all of the time leaves these people burned out and exhausted most of the time. These folks are trapped. Not knowing how to say "no" to others' needs, their only self-protection is to hide from others so they won't notice others' needs!

8) The trainer may ask for a show of hands to indicate the range of scores in the group. She then asks the group to share observations and insights. Some participants may report that their answers to the questions have changed over the years as they have learned to take better care of themselves.

9) The trainer points out the connection between personal belief systems and the addiction to care-giving.

   ● The addiction to helping is the result of well-intentioned but irrational personal beliefs that lead to self-neglect.

   ● Before we can alter our lifestyle and come to grips with our addiction, we need to modify the underlying beliefs that guide our daily decisions.

10) The trainer distributes the **Hooked on Helping Beliefs** worksheet and talks through the three care-giving syndromes. Participants mark for special attention the irrational beliefs that are particularly troublesome to them and complete the bottom portion of the worksheet.

D. Small Group Sharing and Discussion (20–30 minutes)

11) The trainer divides the participants into groups of four people each, or utilizes previously formed sharing groups.

   ➤ Take five minutes each to share insights generated by filling out your **Hooked on Helping Addiction Test** and the **Hooked on Helping Beliefs** worksheet.

   ➤ You may also describe stress-related symptoms you experience as a result of trying to be "everything" to others.

   ➤ The emphasis should be on personal sharing and listening, not advice-giving. Refrain from trying to *help* others. Rather, you should simply listen as carefully as you can, and when your turn comes, share as personally as you are willing.

12) The trainer reconvenes the total group and asks for a few general observations regarding the process.

E. Unraveling the Trap of Addiction (5–10 minutes)

13) Participants are asked—as a total group—to brainstorm a list of strategies for coping with the addiction to care-giving. If the group does not generate many, the trainer may wish to expand on some of the following ideas before closing the session.

- Individual irrational beliefs must be dislodged by countering them with more rational beliefs and expectations. What are some "counters" to each of the *Hooked on Helping Beliefs*.

- **Don't give up the dream of being a care-giver**. It is this very dream that energizes us to reach out to others. Just don't expect to turn your dream into reality 100% of the time, or you'll soon become frustrated, down on yourself and emotionally exhausted.

- **Keep others on your care-giving list, but learn to put your own name on the list as well**. "Love your neighbor as yourself." If you don't care for yourself—God help your neighbor! Neither of you will be cared for!

- **Cultivate assertiveness skills**. Saying "no" when you need to say "no" and "yes" when you need to say "yes," and knowing the difference between the two, is essential to recovery.

- If you're in a real pinch and you don't want to respond to someone else's need, admit that you're a committed member of "Helper's Anonymous." Say, "I'd like to—but you see, I'm a recovering care-giver and I'm not allowed to right now!"

VARIATIONS

- *Helpers Anonymous* (p 118) makes a perfect finale to this exercise!

- If time limitations prohibit the completion of this entire exercise, *Sections B, C,* and *D* can each be shortened or dropped. Each section can stand on its own with minor adaptations. However, the depth of experience participants will gain from a limited version will be lessened accordingly.

- As an addendum to *Section C, Exploring The Trap of Addiction*, the trainer may ask participants to complete the *Burnout Index* (p 25), or the *Stress Symptom Inventory worksheet* (*Stress 1*, p 21). Participants would then be confronted by the draining results of the stress they impose upon themselves when trapped in the addiction to care-giving.

TRAINER'S NOTES

Adapted from Tubesing, Sippel and Loving Tubesing, **Personal Recharging** *(Duluth MN: Whole Person Press, 1981).*

HOOKED ON HELPING ADDICTION TEST

Answer the seven questions below with a *yes* or *no*. Try not to hedge. Choose the answer that's more accurate for you right now.

1) I will almost always listen to others who need   Y   N
    emotional support, but I seldom ask anyone to
    pay attention to my emotional needs.

2) When someone helps me I usually make sure   Y   N
    I do as much or more to help them in return.

3) When I don't respond to someone else's needs,   Y   N
    I often feel selfish.

4) I try hard not to hurt other people's feelings   Y   N

5) Once I say "yes" people can count on me to   Y   N
    get the job done, even if it costs me personally.

6) I avoid conflict whenever possible.   Y   N

7) I tend to get myself in over my head by saying   Y   N
    "yes" too much, too often.

TOTALS   ____   ____

                                                      YES   NO

©1994 Whole Person Press 210 W Michigan Duluth MN 55802   (800) 247-6789

HOOKED ON HELPING BELIEFS

Check yourself against these common care-giving syndromes. How many of these assumptions do you act on? Be aware that rarely do people actually speak these beliefs out loud. Mentally review your behaviors to find out whether you whisper any of these messages to yourself

---

The SUPER-HELPER Syndrome

_____ *I must be everything to everyone.*

_____ *I must be able to help everyone.*

_____ *I don't have the limits of normal people.*

The EMPTY POT Syndrome

_____ *I must always try to help someone if I'm asked.*

_____ *Even though I feel empty, I can always give more.*

_____ *I must never be "out to lunch."*

The YOU FIRST Syndrome

_____ *My needs aren't so important as yours.*

_____ *It's selfish to take care of myself.*

_____ *I'll get my needs met by helping you.*

In what ways do these beliefs lead me into behaviors that cause me distress?

Observations and Comments:

---

47 CIRCUIT OVERLOAD

This assessment tool helps participants to see how much stress they are currently "loading on the circuits."

GOALS

To generate a personal and group list of stressors.

To involve participants in a discussion of the underlying causes of stress.

GROUP SIZE

Unlimited.

TIME FRAME

15–20 minutes

MATERIALS

Circuit Overload worksheets for all participants; blackboard or newsprint easel with markers.

PROCESS

1) The trainer introduces the exercise by describing how each of us is like a circuit box.

   ● When too many things go wrong, we overload the circuit, trip the breaker and lose our power.

2) The trainer distributes the **Circuit Overload** worksheets and asks participants individually to list all the things that currently cause them stress—one in each of the circuit switches.

   ☞ *Explain that this is not a race to see who can overload their circuits first—although this might indicate one cause of stress! Rather it is a tool to start the group thinking about stress in their lives.*

3) The trainer draws one large circuit box on the board. She asks for volunteers to share stressors, writing the responses on the large "group" circuit box.

4) When all the circuits are filled, the trainer invites participants to comment on the patterns they see in this list of stressors, using the questions below to prompt as necessary.

✔ Are the stressors work-related? Family-oriented?

✔ Are they in your control? Out of your control?

✔ Do they involve relationships with others? Financial pressures?

VARIATION

■ After *Step 2*, participants could pair up with a partner and compare lists, looking for common themes in their personal lists. Following this sharing, the trainer would reconvene the group and complete *Step 3* of the exercise.

TRAINER'S NOTES

Submitted by Randy R Weigel.

©1994 Whole Person Press 210 W Michigan Duluth MN 55802   (800) 247-6789

CIRCUIT OVERLOAD

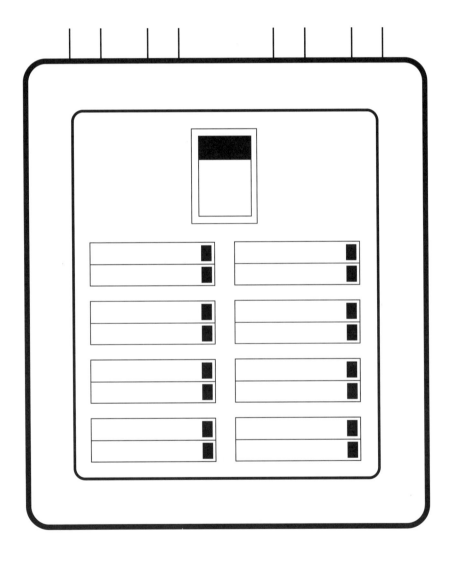

Management
Strategies

48 I'VE GOT RHYTHM

This simple stress management strategy is based on the concept that there's a "right" time for everything. Participants identify the current rhythm of their lives and decide what plans will help them flow with, rather than fight against, their natural rhythm.

GOALS

To illustrate that in stress management, attention to personal timing issues is important.

To help participants identify and act upon their current personal life rhythms.

GROUP SIZE

Unlimited; also effective in work with individuals.

TIME FRAME

15–30 minutes

MATERIALS

My Current Rhythm worksheet for each participant.

PROCESS

1) The trainer points out the relationship between personal rhythms and effective stress management by highlighting the following concepts:

   - Life consists of a variety of rhythms: regular heartbeats, periods of work and sleep, the days, the seasons and the tides. There is a time for everything: a time to mourn and a time to dance, a time to keep silent and a time to speak, a time to weep and a time to laugh, a time to work and a time to play.

   - **Ancient cultures attended carefully to these patterns**. Their sense of timing was highly developed. The Greeks even coined a word for the "right time." They called an opportune moment the *"kairos."* Earlier cultures have known that doing anything at the wrong time created inefficiency and, at times, disaster.

   - Unfortunately, in our culture most of that wisdom has been lost. **Most people are out of touch with their natural rhythm**. Awakened by alarm clocks, eating lunch when their supervisor tells them to, hurrying to finish school, visiting Mother on Sunday afternoon, their natural rhythm is interrupted.

- Resisting one's natural rhythm and sense of timing takes a lot more energy than going with its cadence. Continuously swimming against the flow of your life's current rather than floating with it creates excess stress.

2) The trainer directs participants in an exercise to get in touch with their own personal rhythms.

➤ Please stand up. Try for a moment to become aware of your own rhythm. Start moving in some way (walking, swaying, stretching, bouncing, bending) until you find a style and pace that feels natural, comfortable, familiar. Really tune in to yourself. Do what feels good. Pay attention to your heartbeat, your breathing, your muscle tone, your sense of balance. (2 minutes)

➤ Now, speed up your movement a little bit, then more dramatically. Be aware of how this hurried pace feels. (1 minute)

➤ Return to your natural rhythm now. See how that feels in comparison. (1 minute)

➤ Now slow your pace way down. Be aware of how this slowdown affects your breathing, your balance, your heartbeat. (1 minute)

3) The trainer invites comments from the group on what they experienced in relation to their internal rhythm.

4) The trainer distributes and asks participants to complete the **My Current Rhythm** worksheet.

☞ *Suggest that people work quickly and jot down the first response that comes to mind.*

5) The trainer makes the following suggestion for adjusting stress management plans to fit with the sense of rhythm and personal timing.

- **Pay attention to your personal rhythm**. Let your rhythm guide your actions. Trust your internal wisdom. Attend to your own needs of the moment. If now is a time to be quiet, be quiet. If it's time for you to fight, then fight. If it's a time to play, play wholeheartedly. You can't make jam 'til the strawberries are picked.

- **If you're a "charger,"** always going full bore and forcing yourself to accomplish too much too quickly, then your task is to learn to throttle back to your natural rhythm rather than scrambling to stay ahead of yourself. Your challenge is to listen to the subtle sounds of life within you and swing along with the cadence of that music. If you're worried about missing the boat, remember the Titanic.

- **If you're a "lagger"** who crawls along, hanging back and procrastinating, then you, too, need to listen. There are "right" moments for bold and daring actions. Seize them and go for it.

- **Conserve your energy**. Just ride along through the jolts and delays of life, instead of fighting them. Why not? Your rhythm will carry you.

VARIATIONS

- This process can be utilized as a warm-up preceding an in-depth planning exercise. Participants are urged to take their current life rhythms seriously as they construct their personal plans for change.

- As part of *Step 4*, participants could share insights with each other in their pre-existing small groups or form new groups to discuss "current rhythms."

TRAINER'S NOTES

*Adapted from the **Stress Skills Participant Workbook** (Duluth MN: Whole Person Press, 1977) and **Kicking Your Stress Habits** (Duluth MN: Whole Person Press, 1981).*

TRAINER'S NOTES

MY CURRENT RHYTHM

1) How do you normally respond to the rhythm of your life?
_____ *I'm usually pushing ahead of my own rhythm.*
_____ *I'm usually right in harmony with my own rhythm.*
_____ *I'm usually lagging behind my natural rhythm.*
At this moment I'm _____ *the rhythm of my life.*

(ahead of/behind/right in step with)

2) Use these questions to help identify your natural rhythm at this particular time in your life. Write down the first thought that enters your mind.

Maybe I don't need to be/do _____ *any more.*

(something you need to give up)

Maybe I still need to be/do _____ *some more.*

(something you need to hang on to)

Maybe I need to be/do _____ *sometime soon.*

(a future direction or goal)

Maybe I need to be/do _____ *once again.*

(a past resource or strength to revive)

Maybe I need to be/do _____ *sometimes.*

(something inconsistent or tentative)

Now is the "right time" for you! But what is it the right time for? Look at your answers so far. What is the *"kairos"* for you right now?
Now is the right time for me to _____
_____
_____
_____
_____

3) Take your insights seriously **as** you create a plan for stress management.

Based on my current rhythm, these are some elements I should/ should not include in my stress management plan:

I should include _____   *I should not include* _____
_____   _____
_____   _____
_____   _____
_____   _____

4) Please note: Each time you respond to these questions, your answers will probably be different. Why not? Your rhythm is constantly in flux. Answer these questions again on the 12th day of each month. Then post your answers on the refrigerator door!

©1994 Whole Person Press 210 W Michigan Duluth MN 55802   (800) 247-6789

49 PILEUP COPERS

Using a unique deck of coping cards from the game PILEUP participants gain an overall view of possible coping options and identify their personal coping style, by sorting and discussing both the negative and positive coping cards.

GOALS

To illustrate the difference between positive and negative copers.

To explore the full range of coping options.

To assess personal coping patterns.

GROUP SIZE

Unlimited; also works extremely well in work with individuals and/or family units.

TIME FRAME

60 minutes

MATERIALS

One deck of PILEUP cards for every four participants (available from Whole Person Press); tables for use in sorting and piling cards.

PROCESS

☞ *This exercise is most effective when each participant can sort the cards. However, if you don't have an ample number of PILEUP decks, the exercise can be adapted. Make your own cards or present the copers in a worksheet format.*

1) The trainer introduces the subject of coping with the following concepts:

- Most people cope successfully with 98% of their stressors. We make hundreds of adjustments each day, and manage most situations quite well.

- Usually no single strategy will be effective in managing all of life's challenges. That's why we need a **variety** of coping skills.

- Most people use three or four favorite coping styles over and over again—copers they rely on regularly to get through most tough situations.

2) The trainer instructs participants to think of their three or four favorite, tried and true stress remedies—the ways they cope by habit. Participants then share a few examples with the group.

3) The trainer divides participants into groups of four persons each, and encourages each group to find adequate table space for working together. The trainer then distributes one deck of PILEUP cards to each group with instructions.

➤ Separate the cards by color, keeping the red cards (negative copers) and green cards (positive copers), and setting the yellow cards (stressors) and rainbow cards (creative) aside.

4) The trainer introduces the subject of *negative coping* with the following remarks.

● Every one of your coping mechanisms works to some extent—or you wouldn't use it again! But **some copers have a high cost**. We call these negative copers. Smoking, drinking, and eating **do** bring immediate relief from tension—but the positive effects don't last long and the negative side effects are often quite serious.

● **Most negative copers are effective short-term stress relievers**, but they create additional problems if repeated over a long period of time or in response to many stressors.

5) The trainer gives instructions for exploring negative copers.

➤ Lay out all the negative (red) coping cards on the table and look them over carefully.

➤ Each group member should pick a card representing a negative coper you are likely to use when under great stress

➤ Take turns showing your *negative coper* and sharing with the group *what this coper does for you*, and *what it "costs" you when you use it*.

6) The trainer then introduces the concept of *positive copers.*

● Positive copers are those techniques that are reliable stress relievers without the negative side effects. These skills can be used over and over again for a variety of stressful situations.

● The stack of green PILEUP cards represent some of the many positive coping skills, divided into six major coping strategies or "suits"— physical, emotional, mental, interpersonal, family and diversions.

☞ *The six suits of positive copers (36 skills in all) are outlined below. Take time to review the six different skills in each suit.*

Be sure to point out the symbol used for each category on the
PILEUP cards.

7) The trainer gives instructions for small group discussion of positive
   coping skills.

   ➤ Each person should take a turn sorting the positive copers (green
     cards) into piles that seem **relevant to you**.

   ➤ The person sorting should talk through your decision-making pro-
     cess while you sort.

   ➤ After all the cards are placed in piles, look through each stack and
     share your insights and observations about your coping pattern.

   ➤ Then the next person takes a turn, using your own categories for
     sorting and describing the process out loud as you do it.

   ☞ *You may want to give examples of possible categories (eg,*
      "give myself a grade—A, B, C, D, F" or "use frequently, use
      sometimes, never use" or "appropriate/not appropriate for
      my current stress." But the exercise is most rewarding when
      people make up their own criteria.

8) The trainer raises a few final questions for participants to consider in the
   small groups.

   ✔ Are your commonly-used copers clustered in one category or coping
     suit? Or are they well distributed throughout the suits?

   ✔ Which one or two copers that you don't use now might be the most
     effective additions to your repertoire of coping skills?

   ✔ How might you practice these new copers? In what situations might
     you use them? Against what stressor(s)?

9) The trainer reconvenes the group, collects the cards and asks participants to share their insights and observations.

The colorful **PILEUP** *cards with instructions for 12 additional games are available*
for $15.95 from Whole Person Press. Quantity discounts available on card decks for
use in this exercise. Write or call for a quotation!

The **PILEUP** *cards were originally developed by Whole Person Associates as part*
of THE STRESS KIT © Aid Association for Lutherans, 1982.

PILEUP COPER CARDS*

 ## *NEGATIVE COPERS*

ALCOHOL: Drink to change your mood.
Use alcohol as your friend.

DENIAL: Pretend nothing's wrong. Lie. Ignore
the problem.

DRUGS: Abuse coffee/aspirin/medications.
Smoke pot. Pop pills.

EATING: Keep bingeing. Go on a diet. Use food to
console you.

FAULT FINDING: Have a judgmental attitude. Complain.
Criticize.

ILLNESS: Develop headaches/nervous stomach/
major illness. Become accident prone.

INDULGING: Stay up late. Sleep in. Buy on impulse.
Waste time.

PASSIVITY: Hope it gets better. Procrastinate.
Wait for a lucky break.

REVENGE: Get even. Be sarcastic. Talk mean.

STUBBORNNESS: Be rigid. Demand your way.
Refuse to be wrong.

TANTRUMS: Yell. Mope. Pout. Swear. Drive recklessly.

TOBACCO: Smoke to relieve tension. Smoke to be "in."

WITHDRAWAL: Avoid the situation. Skip school or work.
Keep your feelings to yourself.

WORRYING: Fret over things. Imagine the worst.

*From the **PILEUP** card game,©1982 Aid Association for Lutherans. Available from Whole Person Press.

PILEUP POSITIVE COPERS*

 DIVERSIONS

GETAWAYS:	Spend time alone. See a movie. Daydream.
HOBBIES:	Write. Paint. Remodel. Create something.
LEARNING:	Take a class. Read. Join a club.
MUSIC:	Play an instrument. Sing. Listen to the stereo.
PLAY:	Play a game. Goof off. Go out with friends.
WORK:	Tackle a new project. Keep busy. Volunteer.

 FAMILY

BALANCING:	Balance time at work and home. Accept the good with the bad.
CONFLICT RESOLUTION:	Look for win/win solutions. Forgive readily.
ESTEEM-BUILDING:	Build good family feelings. Focus on personal strengths.
FLEXIBILITY:	Take on new family roles. Stay open to change.
NETWORKING:	Develop friendships with other families. Make use of community resources.
TOGETHERNESS:	Take time to be together. Build family traditions. Express affection.

 INTERPERSONAL

AFFIRMATION:	Believe in yourself. Trust others Give compliments.
ASSERTIVENESS:	State your needs and wants. Say "no" respectfully.
CONTACT:	Make new friends. Touch. Really listen to others.
EXPRESSION:	Show feelings. Share feelings.
LIMITS:	Accept others' boundaries. Drop some involvements.
LINKING:	Share problems with others. Ask for support from family/friends.

*From the **PILEUP** card game,©1982 Aid Association for Lutherans. Available from Whole Person Press.

MORE POSITIVE COPERS

MENTAL

IMAGINATION:	Look for the humor. Anticipate the future.
LIFE PLANNING:	Set clear goals. Plan for the future.
ORGANIZING:	Take charge. Make order Don't let things pile up.
PROBLEM-SOLVING:	Solve it yourself. Seek outside help. Tackle problems head on.
RELABELING:	Change perspectives. Look for good in a bad situation.
TIME MANAGEMENT:	Focus on top priorities. Work smarter, not harder.

PHYSICAL

BIOFEEDBACK:	Listen to your body. Know your physical limitations.
EXERCISE:	Pursue physical fitness. Jog. Swim. Dance. Walk.
NOURISHMENT:	Eat for health. Limit use of alcohol.
RELAXATION:	Tense and relax each muscle. Take a warm bath. Breathe deeply.
SELF-CARE:	Energize your work and play. Strive for self-improvement.
STRETCHING:	Take short stretch breaks throughout your day.

SPIRITUAL

COMMITMENT:	Take up a worthy cause. Say "yes." Invest yourself meaningfully.
FAITH:	Find purpose and meaning. Trust God.
PRAYER:	Confess. Ask forgiveness. Pray for others. Give thanks.
SURRENDER:	Let go of problems. Learn to live with the situation.
VALUING:	Set priorities. Be consistent. Spend time and energy wisely.
WORSHIP:	Share beliefs with others. Put faith into action.

©1994 Whole Person Press 210 W Michigan Duluth MN 55802   (800) 247-6789

TRAINER'S NOTES

50 MONTH OF FUNDAYS

Participants explore the power of play as a stress management strategy and make a plan for incorporating play into their lifestyle every day of the coming month.

GOALS

To promote playfulness as a stress management technique.

To build play into each day's schedule for one month.

GROUP SIZE

Unlimited.

TIME FRAME

20–30 minutes

MATERIALS

Month of Fundays worksheet for all participants.

PROCESS

☞ *The Garden parable (p 113) makes a good introduction or closing for this exercise.*

1) The trainer introduces the exercise with a few brief comments on the importance of play as a stress management strategy.

- **People often get tense because they focus so much on logic, order, production**, etc. Play is meaningless activity that we do just because it feels good! Play allows us an opportunity to indulge our creative, intuitive right brain functions.

- **Play helps us blow off steam and relax** in body, mind and spirit. It also helps us maintain some of our child-like wonder and care-less-ness.

- Play is a form of re-creation that provides a healthy counterbalance to work. **All of us are entitled to guilt-free play time**.

- All work and no play makes Jack or Jill a nervous wreck!

©1994 Whole Person Press 210 W Michigan Duluth MN 55802   (800) 247-6789

2) The trainer invites participants to explore their playfulness.

➤ List 5–10 "playful" activities you engage in regularly or occasionally (eg, surfing, sex, tickling sprees, trips to an amusement park, practical jokes, etc).

➤ Next, recall the wide variety of activities you did for "fun" during childhood or adolescence (eg, flying kites, rolling in the leaves, magic tricks, digging in the mud, riding bikes, throwing stones, kick the can, wrestling, paper dolls, roller skating). List 15–20 different ways you used to play.

3) The **Month of Fundays Calendars** are distributed. As an experiment in stress management, the trainer challenges participants to commit themselves to playing for at least 15 minutes each day during the next month. Participants fill in the calendar, choosing one playful activity for each day from the lists they generated earlier.

☞ *Encourage people to ask their neighbors for suggestions if they get stuck. It's okay to plan the same play activity more than once!*

4) The trainer invites everyone to join in a playful closing activity (eg, a "Hokey Pokey" dance, a rousing chorus of "Boom, Boom, Ain't It Great To Be Crazy," musical chairs, or a giant game of tag).

☞ **Musical Movement *(p 120); Mine-Ha-Ha (Stress 1, p 84); or Pulling Strings (Stress 1, p 124)** would work well.*

VARIATION

■ Invite a number of children to the session as a "panel of experts" on play. Let the kids teach the adults how to play and let them suggest activities for the **Month of Fundays Calendar.**

MONTH OF FUNDAYS

SUNDAY	MONDAY	TUESDAY	WEDNESDAY	THURSDAY	FRIDAY	SATURDAY

51 THE WORRY STOPPER

In this thought-provoking chalktalk and assessment, participants use the criteria of *control* and *importance* to determine what's worth worrying about.

GOALS

To explore the multitudes of things people worry about—both the trivial and the important.

To underline the importance of values in effective stress management.

To provide a tool for deciding what's worth worrying about.

GROUP SIZE

Unlimited; with a large group the trainer will need a movable microphone with a cord long enough to reach into the audience.

TIME FRAME

30–40 minutes

MATERIALS

My Worry List and **The Worry Stopper** worksheets for all participants.

PROCESS

1) The trainer introduces the exercise by asking the group for a show of hands in response to the questions:

   ✔ How many people never worry?

   ✔ Who here is an expert on worrying?

2) The trainer moves out into the audience with a microphone (Donahue style) and asks some of the expert worriers what, specifically, they worry about.

   ☞ *Stay with one person until he "runs dry!" You may need to prime the pump periodically with leading questions like, "What are you worrying about right now?" "What does your spouse worry about?" "Your kids?" "Your parents?" The idea is to generate a wide range of worries—both trivial and profound—from each person.*

3) After 5 or 6 people have shared their worries, the trainer distributes the **Worry List** worksheets to everyone and challenges them to write down everything they worry about, using the prompting questions on the worksheet to help trigger their awareness.

> ☞ *You may want to elaborate, giving more examples of the kinds of things people might worry about (eg, "Does my breath smell?" "Did I unplug the coffee pot?" "Is my son using drugs?" "Am I pregnant?" "Did the gas bill come?" "Will I be able to afford a new coat?" "Will my tires last the winter?" "Will there be a drought this year?" "Will I have any cavities?" "Will I get stuck in the elevator?" "Will Social Security be bankrupt when I get there?" "Can I lose 10 pounds by summer?" etc).*

4) The trainer comments that there seem to be lots of worrying experts here after all! She goes on to make some general observations about worry and stress, covering some or all of the points outlined below.

- **Most people are astounded at the number of life situations they are worried about at a given moment in time.** Usually these worries lurk at the edges of our awareness until some stimulus brings one or more into focus.

- **Worrying is a useless waste of energy unless it motivates us** to take some action to deal with the perceived threat.

- Some experts estimate that up to **95% of our stress reactions are in response to the trivial** rather than the important events in life. This process results from faulty perceptions and murky values that lead us to worry unnecessarily.

- Rather than deciding clearly what's worth worrying about, we all too often end up in the same boat with the anonymous worrier who penned these lines:

> *It's the little things that bother*
> *and keep you on the rack;*
> *You can sit upon a mountain*
> *but not upon a tack!*

- Some recent studies suggest that **the distinction between eustress and distress may be primarily determined by our perception of control.** If we feel in control, even an extremely anxiety-provoking situation may be seen as challenging rather than distressful. If we feel powerless, even the most trivial worry can be distressing.

- **The key to effective stress management is to worry wisely**—to spend our energy on the things we truly value and those we can control.

5) The trainer distributes the **Worry Stopper** worksheets and invites participants to diagnose their own worry patterns.

➤ Look over your list and transfer each item to the appropriate panel of the **Worry Stopper** based on your answers to these questions:

    ➣ Is this really important to me?

    ➣ Is this in my control?

➤ Worries that are *important to you AND in your control* should be transferred to *Panel I* of the **Worry Stopper**.

➤ Worries that are *important but NOT in your control* are written in *Panel II*. *Panel III* is for worries that are *NOT important and NOT in your control.*

➤ Worries that are *in your control but are NOT important* are placed in *Panel IV*.

6) The trainer asks participants to examine their entries in each panel and at the bottom of the worksheet jot down whatever general comments strike them about the panel and the worries it contains.

7) The trainer reviews the panels one at a time, soliciting input from the group as she reviews appropriate coping strategies for each.

- **Panel I.** Since these items are *important to us and also in our control*, they are certainly worth worrying about—especially if our concern motivates us to get moving on needed change. However, if this panel is filled to overflowing, we may need to reconsider how important each of these items really is. Relabeling skills might help us move some of these worries into *Panel IV*.

- **Panel II.** Since these items are *important, but not in our control*, we either need to gain some control and move the worry to *Panel I* or use our surrender skills. If we truly cannot change the situation, we need to let go!

- **Panel III.** It's surprising how many life situations we worry about that are *neither in our control nor really important to us*. Why waste an ounce of our precious energy on these items? Why not cross them off the worry list right now!

- **Panel IV.** If the items in this panel are *not really important to us*, we need to ask ourselves whether they are worth fretting about. It's amazing how much time and energy we spend working on trivia just because we can control it. Why worry about or try to change something that's not really important?

8) The trainer helps participants generate their personal **Worry Stopper** plan.

 ➤ *Circle* one item in each panel that *you want to stop worrying about.*

 ➤ For each choice, *write a brief description of how you will accomplish the goal* (eg, "I'm going to go have this lump checked." "Every time the thought of rising taxes crosses my mind, I'll say 'let the governor worry about it!'" "Instead of worrying about whether my spouse is an alcoholic, I'll start going to Alanon," etc).

9) The trainer invites volunteers to stand up and read one or more of their worry-stopping resolutions.

 ☞ *The trainer may want to close this exercise with the **Treasure Chest Fantasy** (p 132) or one of the skill-builders from **I Surrender!** (Stress 1, p 78).*

TRAINER'S NOTES

We learned this technique from Fay Zachary at the First Annual Conference on Burnout in Philadelphia.

©1994 Whole Person Press 210 W Michigan Duluth MN 55802   (800) 247-6789

THE WORRY LIST

List everything you worry about—big things, little things, anything that causes you concern or makes you uneasy.

Be sure to include worries about:

- ■ *Personal* health and well-being, comfort, success, safety, behavior.

- ■ Immediate and extended *family* health, finances, changes.

- ■ *Job-related concerns*, people performance, future.

- ■ Neighborhood and *community issues,* taxes, politics, schools.

- ■ Ultimate *life questions.*

- ■ *Global issues*, war, natural resources, human rights.

- ■ *Trivia*, the little things that bother.

MY WORRY LIST

_____

_____

_____

_____

_____

_____

_____

_____

_____

_____

_____

_____

_____

_____

_____

_____

_____

_____

_____

_____

_____

THE WORRY STOPPER

	I CAN Control	I CAN'T Control	
Important To Me			**Important To Me**
	I	**II**	
	IV	**III**	
NOT Important To Me			**NOT Important To Me**
	I CAN Control	I CAN'T Control	

OBSERVATIONS:

Panel I

Panel II

Panel III

Panel IV

52 CONSULTANTS UNLIMITED

Participants act as a consultation team engaged to devise alternative strategies for managing each others' "on-the-job" stressors.

GOALS

To generate and evaluate coping strategies for specific job stressors.

To reinforce the concept of peer consultation as a problem-solving model.

GROUP SIZE

Described for 10–30 participants; can be adapted for larger groups.

TIME FRAME

5–10 minutes for each consultation; 30–45 minutes in all.

MATERIALS

One or more 3"x5" index cards for each person; newsprint.

PROCESS

1) The trainer distributes 3"x5" cards to participants and asks everyone to describe briefly on the card one source of stress in their work setting.

   ☞ *Reassure the group that all stress "entries" will remain anonymous. If people in the group know each other well, suggest a few guidelines participants may use to protect themselves in their work setting:*

   Phrase your stressor in general terms.
   Do not use names.
   Keep the focus on how you experience the stress rather than blaming, judging or complaining.

   If the group is small (less than 15 people), encourage participants to submit 2 or 3 stressors so the pool is larger and more anonymous.

2) The trainer collects the stressor cards, selects one (either at random or because it is "typical") and reads it to the group; she invites everyone to join the consultation team by imagining alternative ways to deal with the stress. The group brainstorms strategies that might be helpful in coping with that specific job situation. Each suggestion is recorded on the newsprint. (3 minutes)

3) The group is asked to decide on the three best strategies among those listed. (2 minutes)

☞ *The point here is to identify several workable coping plans. There is no magic in choosing three—two or four will do fine.*

4) The trainer chooses another job stressor for consultation. *Steps 2* and *3* are repeated using a clean newsprint to record management alternatives for this stressor.

5) The group continues to consult using this model until their energy flags or suggestions get repetitive. The trainer invites participants to comment on their insights and learnings from this process.

☞ *At the end of the session, participants may want to claim the brainstorm newsprint referring to their job situation.*

VARIATION

■ Participants could be divided into 3 or 4 person consultation teams who brainstorm strategies for dealing with each others' stressful job situations.

TRAINER'S NOTES

TRAINER'S NOTES

Skill Builders

53 ATTITUDE ADJUSTMENT HOUR

In this lively exercise participants practice the art of altering their viewpoint by telling and retelling the stories of their day from different perspectives.

GOALS

To demonstrate the role of perception in the management of stress.

To help participants practice making conscious shifts in their perceptual patterns.

GROUP SIZE

Unlimited; also works well in family counseling.

TIME FRAME

25–35 minutes

MATERIALS

Accident Reports reading.

PROCESS

1) The trainer emphasizes the role of perception in both the creation of stress and its successful management, by outlining the following concepts:

   ● Any life event, major or minor, can become a cause of stress if we view it as a threat. Stress is our reaction to whatever dangers we see around us. Perception is the key to stress management. Our stress level is determined by the way we label events (perception). If we see "safety" we remain relaxed. If we see "danger" we fight back with stress.

   ● Incredible as it sounds,**most of our stress comes from between our ears.** If we don't like it, we can get rid of it, by changing our mind.

   ● It's no more phoney to be "Pollyanna-ish" (seeing the rosy side of very tough problems) than it is to be cynical (seeing the negative side of positive opportunities).

- **At any given moment, we always have numerous perceptual options available to us**—many ways to view our situations. Our choices of viewpoints, to a large extent, color the quality and feeling tone of our daily experiences.

- In our society "attitude adjustment hour" is synonymous with drinking alcohol. Yes, alcohol does alter people's mood. **But true attitude adjustment comes only from making the choice to change our perception.** This exercise offers an opportunity for you to practice the skill of seeing your life from many different possible viewpoints.

2) The trainer directs participants to find partners. Each person in the dyad takes two minutes to describe her day to her partner. (4 minutes total)

☞ *If this exercise is being used early in the day, ask participants to describe yesterday.*

3) The trainer tells participants that in a few moments they will be challenged to "adjust their attitudes" and re-describe their days using a different viewpoint. He outlines the eight alternate perspectives they could potentially use, writing each suggestion on the board as it is described:

➤ Re-tell the story of your day *as if it were* . . .

   ➤ A SITUATION COMEDY—a big joke and the joke is on you.

   ➤ A GREEK TRAGEDY—as if you were meant to suffer and you surely did.

   ➤ A SOAP OPERA—of heroic proportions, with all the subtlety, intrigue and drama of the tube.

   ➤ A FAIRYTALE—perfectly positive and enjoyable, everything rosy.

   ➤ A BORE—no expressions, dull, ho-hum, nothing much interesting.

   ➤ AN ATHLETIC CONTEST—using sports metaphors as you "drive for the goal," "take a time out," "strike out," "hit an ace," etc.

   ➤ A PITIFUL MESS—you're lousy and you mess everything up, and your life stinks.

   ➤ A TRAP—everyone's out to get you and you have a lot to complain about.

☞ *This is a good time to read a sampling of the Accident Reports statements. The laughter generated by these absurd attitude adjustments should stimulate the group's creativity.*

4) The trainer gives instructions for story telling.

> ☞ *Encourage participants to be as dramatic as possible in their descriptions and to really "get into" the chosen viewpoint.*

➤ The **older person** in each pair should choose one of the altered perspectives and re-describe your day to your partner using that viewpoint.

➤ Then the younger partner should choose a **different** viewpoint, adjust your attitude, and re-tell the story of your day from this new perspective.

➤ You will each have 2 minutes. I will let you know when to switch roles.

5) *Step 4* is repeated two or three times, allowing both partners an opportunity to re-view their day from several perspectives.

6) The trainer reconvenes the group. Participants are asked to consider and comment on the following questions:

✔ How did the changed viewpoint alter your feelings?

✔ How do you normally choose to tell your day's story?

✔ What difference would it make in your life if you regularly sat down at the end of the day for an "attitude adjustment hour" in which you told and retold your day's story from different perspectives?

✔ How can you incorporate the principles of perception into your day right while it's happening?

VARIATION

■ Instead of instructing participants to retell their day "as if it were . . ." the trainer may suggest that participants retell their day from someone else's perspective. (2 minutes each)

➤ "How would your day be described by . . ."

    ➣ Your boss/supervisor/subordinate?

    ➣ Your spouse?

    ➣ Your kids/parents?

    ➣ An investigative reporter from TV news?

    ➣ A neighbor?

    ➣ People you serve (clients, customers, parishioners)?

ACCIDENT REPORTS*

- Coming home, I drove into the wrong house and collided with a tree I didn't have.

- The other car collided with mine without even giving warning of its intentions.

- I collided with a stationary truck coming the other way.

- A truck backed through my windshield into my wife's face.

- A pedestrian hit me and went under my car.

- The guy was all over the road. I had to swerve a number of times before I hit him.

- I pulled away from the side of the road, glanced at my mother-in-law, and headed for the embankment.

- As I approached the intersection a sign suddenly appeared in a place where no sign had ever appeared before. I was unable to stop in time to avoid the accident.

- To avoid hitting the car in front of me, I struck the pedestrian.

- In my attempt to hit a fly, I drove into a telephone pole.

- My car was legally parked and it backed into the other vehicle.

- I told the police that I was not injured, but upon removing my hat, I found that I had a fractured skull.

- The pedestrian had no idea which direction to run, so I ran over him.

- The indirect cause of this accident was a little guy in a small car with a big mouth.

- An invisible car came out of nowhere, struck my vehicle and vanished.

- I had been driving for forty years when I fell asleep at the wheel.

- I saw a sad-faced old gentleman as he glanced off of the hood of my car.

- I was thrown from my car as it left the road. I was later found in a ditch by some stray cows.

- The telephone pole was approaching. I was attempting to swerve out of the way when it struck my front end.

- I was on my way to the doctor with rear end trouble when my universal joint gave way causing me to have an accident.

Each of these is an actual statement gleaned from official accident reports submitted to police and insurance investigators.

©1994 Whole Person Press 210 W Michigan Duluth MN 55802   (800) 247-6789

54 SPEAK UP!

Participants explore the value of assertiveness as a coping skill by pairing up and experimenting with alternative styles both for making requests and for saying "no."

GOALS

To assess personal comfort and skill in asking for things and in saying "no."

To learn the difference between effective and ineffective requests and refusals.

To practice assertive direct expression of requests and refusals.

GROUP SIZE

Unlimited.

TIME FRAME

40–45 minutes

MATERIALS

Newsprint easel or blackboard.

PROCESS

1) The trainer introduces the general concept of assertiveness and under- lines the importance of assertiveness as a coping skill.

- It's amazing how much stress we could eliminate from our lives by practicing two simple techniques—**saying "no"** (to unrewarding activities, extra obligations, inappropriate requests, etc), and **asking directly** for what we want. Making direct requests of others and turning down requests from others are two components of **assertive** behavior.

- Most of us stress ourselves and the people around us with our style of making requests and of giving responses to others' requests. All too often, people are either so passive that others have to guess at their meaning, or so aggressive that others feel the sting of their anger. **Neither the non-assertive nor the aggressive pattern is a very effective style of communicating**.

● **Non-assertive people have difficulty asking for things directly**. They tend to either avoid asking, or they ask in such an indirect, self-effacing way that their requests are often not understood, or are easily turned down. Likewise, when they say "no," they tend to be indirect and give excuses instead of stating the real reasons for their hesitation. Non-assertive people are also easily persuaded to do what they don't want to do. These non-assertive behaviors are a sure-fire source of stress for both the requester and the responder.

● **Aggressive people tend to be the opposite**. They will make requests willingly and say "no" clearly, but do so in a manner that tends to be coercive, hostile, demanding and disrespectful. Such behavior is also often stressful to both giver and receiver.

2) The trainer asks participants to give examples of both non-assertive and aggressive ways to make and refuse requests.

☞ *You may want to role play several examples with the class.*

The book, How To Make Yourself Miserable by Dan Greenberg, includes some wonderful cynical dialogues demonstrating how to make sure your request is rejected. These amusing vignettes could be read by the trainer to add humor, since they are guaranteed to solicit empathic chuckles from the group.

3) The trainer asks participants to recall personal examples.

➤ Note a recent stressful incident when someone requested something from you and you had difficulty saying "no."

➤ Remember and note another recent experience when you felt under stress about asking for something you wanted.

4) **Making a reasonable request; saying "no."** The trainer asks group members to form pairs.

➤ Decide who will be the *asker* and who will be the *refuser*.

➤ The *asker* should think of a series of reasonable requests that you can make of the other person (eg, "I'd like a hug," or "Tell me what you think of me," or "Could I borrow a quarter for the phone," etc).

➤ The *refuser* should respond with one word only: "no."

When everyone understands the instructions clearly, the trainer tells the pairs to begin the request and refusal process, keeping it up for three minutes. At the end of that time, the pairs reverse roles and repeat this activity for another three minutes. (6 minutes)

5) While allowing people to stay with their partners, the trainer solicits a brief discussion from the entire group concerning their reactions to doing this exercise.

☞ *Participants usually express feelings of discomfort at being limited to saying "no." You will need to help them clarify what else they want to communicate to the **asker** besides "no." People often want to explain why they are saying "no," or want to let the **asker** know they are willing to say "yes" at another time. **Requesters** may feel hurt or put off by the abruptness and finality of a "no" answer.*

6) **Saying "no" with phoney excuses; making alternative requests.** The trainer tells the pairs to continue with a similar routine.

➤ This time the *refusers* are to make up phoney excuses about why you can't do what is being asked. Your task is to avoid revealing your real reason for saying "no."

➤ The *asker* is to be very persistent, and to *offer alternatives* and/or solutions to the refuser's excuses.

☞ *You could briefly role play this activity with another person.*

7) Pairs experiment with this *request and phoney excuse* sequence for 2–3 minutes. When the trainer calls time, partners switch roles and repeat the exercise for 2–3 minutes. (6 minutes)

☞ *Refusers usually find that the **asker's** persistence in countering their excuses makes it very difficult for them to continue making the excuses. Participants discover that the search for more and more excuses usually generates an anxious "scrambling" plus a feeling of discomfort at being dishonest.*

Sometimes participants will ask for advice on how to deal with the person whose feelings are hurt by the refusal, and the group as a whole can think of assertive ways to show concern and caring for the person without giving up on their decision to say "no."

Remind participants that they can choose to honestly explain why they are refusing the request, but they don't have to justify their actions.

If there is time, the group may discuss some of the reasons why they are afraid to ask for what they want, or hesitant to say "no" (eg, "They won't like me anymore," or "I'll hurt his feelings," or "I'll be obligated to her," etc).

8) **Assertive requests and refusals**. In the third and final part of this exercise, the pairs continue to make and refuse requests.

➤ Take turns making requests and refusing, but this time the *refuser* uses one of three assertive responses:

➢ *"No I won't"* or *"No I don't want to"* (no explanation).

➢ *"No . . . because"* (with an honest explanation).

➢ *"No . . . but"* (with possible alternatives).

➤ When both people have practiced making and refusing requests assertively, give each other feedback as to how assertive you were in each role. (10 minutes or more)

9) The trainer asks the entire group to briefly discuss what it was like both to make assertive requests and to experience the clear refusals in *Step 7*. The group generates a list of situations in which these skills would be particularly effective.

10) Participants are encouraged to keep practicing honestly saying "no" (with and without explanation) in their private and/or professional lives whenever they have the opportunity.

● Once you grow comfortable saying "no," it will probably be easier for you to ask for what you want directly and also to say an unqualified "yes" when you do want to accept.

VARIATION

■ As part of *Step 8*, participants could use the skills they have practiced in this exercise by role playing with their partners more effective and assertive ways of handling their personal list of stressful *requests* and *refusals* which they identified in *Step 3*.

*Submitted by Sandy Christian who adapted this process from an exercise in Lange and Jakubowski's **Responsible Assertive Behavior** (Champaign IL: Research Press, 1976).*

55 AFFIRMATIVE ACTION PLAN

In this attitude-changing exercise participants draw up a plan for using affirmation to manage a workplace stressor.

GOALS

To explore the potential of affirmation as a stress management skill.

To increase participants' repertoire of affirming behaviors.

To develop on-the-job applications for affirmation skills.

GROUP SIZE

Unlimited.

TIME FRAME

40–50 minutes

MATERIALS

Blackboard or flipchart; **Affirmative Action Plan** worksheets for all participants.

PROCESS

1) The trainer gives some background information on affirmation as a stress reducer, covering some or all of the following points:

   - **Affirmation is a basic human need**. Everyone needs to be recognized, appreciated and touched by other people. Eric Berne popularized this concept by calling it *stroke hunger*.

   - **Many work settings are characterized by a highly competitive system** where excellence is expected and compliments are few and far between. The need for affirmation or appreciation may be seen as a sign of weakness. Interactions may be calculated to put each other down rather than build each other up. What a pity! There's no substitute for the glow that comes from hearing directly, person-to-person, that you are liked, valued and appreciated by your co-workers.

   - **Appreciation is often a more influential motivator than pay**. Most of us will really "put out" just in order to hear someone say, "thank you." The phenomenal success of *The One Minute Manager* is based in part on a simple challenge to managers: "Sneak around and catch people doing something good, then tell them about it!"

● Hans Selye, the pioneer stress researcher contends that **revenge is the most stressful emotion—and gratitude is the healthiest.** His personal prescription for managing stress includes cultivating a positive attitude and making every day a thanksgiving day.

● **Cultivating the attitude of gratitude is a double-duty stress management strategy.** Your positive attitude will reduce the stress for the people around you—and probably will reduce your stress as well. As an added bonus, appreciation seems to be contagious— once we start giving it freely, it often comes back to us full circle.

2) The trainer distributes **Affirmative Action Plan** worksheets to everyone and invites participants to think of someone in their work setting who could benefit from some additional affirmation (eg, someone you have difficulty relating to; someone you don't particularly like; someone who is under a lot of stress or creates a lot of stress).

➤ Write down the name of your chosen co-worker at the top of the worksheet.

She invites the group to follow along as she leads them through a process designed to help them put a little sunshine in that person's life.

3) The trainer introduces the first aspect of the plan, *acknowledgment*, asking the group for ideas about how they might simply acknowledge a person's presence or existence. All suggestions are listed on the blackboard or newsprint. The trainer elaborates as necessary, categorizes the responses into three strategies, and challenges participants to imagine how they could apply them.

● **Make non-verbal contact** (eg, eye contact, smile, sit nearby, touch, etc).

● **Make verbal contact** (eg, say "hello," initiate a conversation, tell a joke, ask a question, etc).

● **Pay attention** (eg, listen respectfully, ask for input, respond to his verbal/non-verbal offerings, etc).

➤ Now apply these techniques to your situation and write down in the *Acknowledge* section of your worksheet all the potential ways to acknowledge your chosen person.

☞ *This should be a time for idea-generating, not making commitments. Encourage participants to list **all** actions they **could** take, not just those options they want to or are willing to carry out. Remind the group to be specific about how, where, when and how often they could acknowledge this person.*

4) The trainer invites participants to consider the next aspect of their plan—**affirmation**, which according to Webster means "responding to in a positive manner" or "to confirm." The trainer goes on to suggest some basic affirmation techniques.

   ● Everyone has some redeeming qualities—so spend enough time interacting with this person to **discover his strengths**.

   ● **Focus on the positive**, find something to like about this person.

   ● **Reinforce what you like,** however insignificant—then disregard everything else.

   The trainer challenges the group to think of appropriate phrases that could communicate affirmation (eg, "I see what you mean," "That's a good idea," "What an interesting viewpoint," "Tell me more about that!"). After several suggestions are generated, participants apply them to their situation.

   ➤ Now complete the *Affirm* section on your worksheet, answering the questions and identifying specific ways you could *affirm* your co-worker.

5) The trainer invites participants to explore yet another type of affirmative action—**encouragement**, which literally means "to give courage," but more often is interpreted as "giving support." The trainer asks for illustrations of how group members like to be supported by asking:

   ✔ What can other people do for/to you that builds you up, strengthens you, gives you hope, courage or support?

   Participants give examples of ways they like to be encouraged and the phrases that might accompany such gestures of support (eg, "You did so well last time, this will be a breeze," "I know you can do it!" "You're such a kind soul!" "You've learned a lot about how to handle this," etc).

   ➤ Turn the tables, now and apply what you know about your own need for *encouragement* to the person you've chosen to affirm. Write your responses and potential plans in the *Encourage* section of the worksheet.

©1994 Whole Person Press 210 W Michigan Duluth MN 55802   (800) 247-6789

6) The trainer introduces the next dimension of affirmative action, ***appreciation***, by giving several honest compliments to the group or individual participants (eg, "I've appreciated your willingness to share," "This is one of the liveliest groups I've worked with," "I've noticed that John has helped us stay on track when we wander—I appreciate your clarity, John.")

The trainer points out some tips for showing appreciation:

- Compliments or praise can show appreciation for another person's strengths, appearance, accomplishments, behavior, special gifts.

- To be most effective, such positive feedback should be **stated directly** to the recipient (eg, "Stuart, your report was excellent!").

- The best messages of appreciation are also **specific**, giving details about the quality, behavior or accomplishment you're praising (eg, not only "Your report was excellent," but also "it was concise, clearly organized, and well-documented—your choice of words got the point across without offending anyone").

- The impact of a compliment is increased by including a statement about **how the behavior affected you** (eg, "I felt proud of our whole team when you were done—your presentation reminded me how well we cooperated together").

- Nobody ever really gets tired of hearing honest compliments, so feel free to show your appreciation **frequently**.

➤ Again consider your chosen co-worker and write down in the ***Appreciation*** section several ways you could show your *appreciation* openly to that person.

7) The trainer directs participants' attention to the fifth method of affirmation, **thanks-giving**. She notes that all of us have much to be thankful for and asks participants to give examples of things in their work setting for which they are grateful (eg, coffee pot, flexible hours, secretary who can spell, camaraderie of staff, Christmas party, electric pencil sharpener, etc).

The trainer notes that even the office ogre makes some contributions that are deserving of thanks.

- As with appreciation, **gratitude is most effective when it is direct, specific and frequent**. People love to be thanked over and over again for big favors and small kindnesses.

- Contrary to popular belief, there's nothing wrong with buttering up the boss—or the errand boy. In fact, it's likely to be healthy for both of you!

➤ List the various reasons for saying *"thank you"* to your chosen co-worker.

8) The trainer instructs participants to look over their list of "coulds" and circle (or mark with a star) those affirmative actions they are actually willing to implement. These commitments are revised and rewritten as statements, "I will . . ."

9) Participants are invited to share with the group one or more of their affirmation commitments. The trainer reinforces all suggestions, modeling affirmative action and using these contributions to summarize important points of the session.

☞ *Closing process designs like* **Manager Of The Year** *(p 98),* **Vital Signs(Wellness 2,** *p 109) and* **Coping Skills Affirmations** *(***Stress 1**, *p 110) give participants an additional opportunity to practice appreciation with each other.*

VARIATIONS

■ After *Step 8*, participants could pair up or rejoin small groups and describe their affirmation plan. Listeners practice their own affirmation skills by giving positive feedback and support.

■ Participants make two affirmative action plans—one for a coworker and one for a family member or friend. The group may want to discuss the difference in their affirmation patterns at home versus on the job.

■ Participants could use this same process to make an affirmative action plan for themselves, complete with ideas on how to acknowledge, affirm, encourage, appreciate and thank themselves each day.

■ As part of *Step 6*, participants could practice giving compliments to others in the group, stating their appreciation for another person's *being, doing* or *sharing* and elaborating with details.

AFFIRMATIVE ACTION PLAN

My plan for affirming _____

ACKNOWLEDGE

In what ways could you let this person know more clearly that you know she/he is living, breathing, exists, etc? What little things could you do to pay attention to this person?

I could . . .

AFFIRM

How and when could you respond in a positive manner to this person? What thoughts, opinions, beliefs, does she/he hold that you could confirm as true? What positive phrases could you use more often?

I could . . .

ENCOURAGE

In what ways could you give this person support even if you're in disagreement? What might enhance this person's self-confidence? What does she/he need to hear to feel strengthened to tackle the day?

I could . . .

AFFIRMATIVE ACTION PLAN, continued

APPRECIATE

What are some of this person's strengths that you value? When could you honestly praise him/her? What compliments could you give?

I could . . .

GIVE THANKS

What contributions does this person make for which you are grateful? When could you say "thank you"?

I could . . .

AFFIRMITIVE ACTION PLAN

I will . . .

©1994 Whole Person Press 210 W Michigan Duluth MN 55802   (800) 247-6789

56 ANCHORING

Participants guide one another through a soothing relaxation fantasy and "anchor" the comfortable feelings they experience for later recall and stimulation of the relaxation response.

GOALS

To develop a quick self-eliciting resource for relaxation.

To demonstrate the potency of recalled experience in evoking relaxation responses.

GROUP SIZE

Unlimited.

TIME FRAME

30 minutes

MATERIALS

A copy of **Instructions for Guides** and **Instructions for Followers** for each participant.

PROCESS

1) The trainer describes the relationship between stress and relaxation using the S–R model outlined below:

   ● The stress response is elicited by whatever cues we perceive as threatening (eg, a near-accident, a noise in a dark house, a final exam). Even past experiences we recall or fantasy experiences that never occurred can elicit the stress response.

   ● **The relaxation response is also stimulated by certain cues** (eg, music, watching the ocean, lying in the sun, a soothing touch, etc). The relaxation response can also be elicited by past experiences we recall and by fantasy experiences that we imagine.

   ● **Each individual is free to choose which cues to attend to.** We can choose to respond to cues that elicit relaxation rather than cues that promote stress. We can also purposefully train ourselves to relax in response to a specific cue.

2) The trainer explains the purpose of the exercise—to connect a series of relaxing experiences/images to a spot on the body. This process is called **anchoring**. Subsequently touching this spot acts as a cue for eliciting the relaxation response.

3) Participants pair up and distribute themselves around the room. Partners will be training one another in the anchoring technique.

4) The trainer distributes the **Instructions for Guides** and **Instructions for Followers** to all participants. One partner is the **guide** first. The other partner is the *follower*. The trainer briefly describes the process, then allows the pairs to read their instructions thoroughly. The trainer answers any questions and then directs participants to proceed at their own pace.

☞ *Wander around the room quietly offering assistance or clarification as needed.*

5) After 10 minutes, the trainer signals the **guides** that time is up. The partners debrief and check the anchoring response as indicated on their instructions. Then they change roles and repeat the process. (10–15 minutes)

☞ *Be sure to allow time for the **followers** to describe their experience to their partners before switching roles and moving on.*

6) When all participants have completed the practice, the trainer may reconvene the group and ask people to share their experiences. (5 minutes)

7) Participants are encouraged to "pile up" even more experiences on the anchor by touching it whenever they feel particularly relaxed (eg, hot bath, sunset, sitting by the fire).

VARIATION

■ A related technique called *spot checking* uses a visual cue to elicit relaxation. The process for *spot checking* remains as outlined above for *anchoring* except participants in this case anchor the relaxation experience visually to a small colored adhesive dot (available at office supply stores). The dots are then placed by the person at strategic locations (phone, typewriter, watch, wallet) as a visual reminder to relax.

Submitted by David X Swenson.

ANCHORING

INSTRUCTIONS FOR FOLLOWERS

1) Your guide is going to help you visualize a series of especially relaxing scenes from your personal experience or fantasy.

2) During this experience you will need a *silent signal* to communicate with your partner. Just *nod your head* to let him know when you have an image clearly in mind and are experiencing peak relaxation.

3) You also need to choose a *spot on your body* for your partner to use as *an "anchor" point* for these relaxation visualizations.

   Most people choose a spot near the knuckle of the index finger. Your guide will touch this spot for you when you indicate peak relaxation. Later you can touch this same spot to elicit feelings of relaxation for yourself.

4) You will be visualizing two or three scenes.

   Each time you feel yourself relaxing totally into the mood of the scene you will nod to your guide and he will touch you on the anchor spot. This will add each subsequent relaxation experience to those already "anchored" to that spot.

5) When your time is up, describe your experience as completely as you can, paying special attention to the signs of relaxation you notice.

6) *Before you switch roles* and become the guide, touch your anchor spot yourself and notice the response.

7) Remember, you can add more of your own calming experiences to this special spot by touching your anchor point whenever you're feeling particularly relaxed. Then, when you're under stress, just take a deep breath, touch the anchor point and the relaxing images will again flood into your being.

ANCHORING

INSTRUCTIONS FOR GUIDES

1) Begin by asking your partner to show you the exact spot she wants you to use as an "anchor" for her relaxed feelings.

2) Ask your partner to *find a comfortable, balanced posture* (seated, lying, leaning against the wall).

   Once she is settled ask her to *take a deep breath, close her eyes and relax.* Tell her to *focus on breathing and let go of any tension she feels.* Instruct her to *continue breathing deeply and to nod her head when she feels quite relaxed.*

3) As soon as she nods her head, you are going to help her recall an especially relaxing experience. Your job is to help her make it vivid in her imagination. Your instructions need to guide her in the process, yet be general enough so that she can create the scene for herself.

   You will need to go slowly, allowing time for the images to form in her mind. A nod is always a signal that she is ready to move on.

4) Start by saying: *I'd like you to recall a deeply relaxing situation from your personal experience, a time when you felt extremely calm and at peace. Remember everything you can about that time of peaceful relaxation. Bring it alive in your mind.*

   While your partner is imaging, you can heighten the sensory visualization by suggesting she *notice the colors, hues, shapes and contrasts in her image.*

   After a pause you might suggest that she *pay attention to the sounds and smells, the temperature, the feeling of the scene around her.*

   All these suggestions should be made in very general terms so your partner can create the specifics of her scenario without your preferences sneaking in. Try permissive language such as *you might notice.* Use words suggesting relaxation such as *restful, comfortable, easy, calm, peaceful.*

5) When the experience is quite realistic and eliciting peak relaxation, your partner should nod. At this point, you should touch her "anchor spot."

6) Ask your partner to *recall another relaxing experience or ask her to create in fantasy the most relaxing scene she could possibly imagine.* Repeat *Steps 4 and 5,* helping her enrich the scene with sensory images and anchoring the response to her "spot" when the experience is most intense.

7) Repeat *Step 4 and Step 5* with a third relaxation fantasy.

8) Ask your partner to *return her awareness outside herself again, back to your interaction.* Give her a minute or two to get reoriented and then ask her to describe her experience to you.

9) Sometime during her description reach over and touch the "anchor spot" to test if it really elicits relaxation.

©1994 Whole Person Press 210 W Michigan Duluth MN 55802   (800) 247-6789

57 THE ABC'S OF TIME

This skill-building exercise illustrates the importance of spending time where it counts. Participants list the activities and tasks that consumed yesterday's 24 hours, then assess whether or not they invested effort in their top priorities.

GOALS

To help participants identify how they spend their time.

To distinguish the "A" priorities from the "B" and "C" tasks.

To understand and practice the major time-use skills.

GROUP SIZE

Unlimited.

TIME FRAME

40–50 minutes

MATERIALS

A copy of **Yesterday's Time Log Analysis** for each participant; **Each Day is a New Account** script.

PROCESS

A. Time-Use Analysis (25–30 minutes)

1) The trainer distributes **Yesterday's Time Log Analysis** worksheets and instructs participants to complete *Columns I* and *II*. (10 minutes)

   ➤ Mentally think through the details of your schedule yesterday—what you did, when, who you talked with, about what, etc. Be as precise as possible in recalling the specifics of your day and try to list every activity in *Column 1*.

   ☞ *Encourage people to be very specific and detailed by giving a host of examples (eg, ate breakfast, brushed teeth, picked up kitchen, dictation, read magazine, watched TV, talked with the kids, staff meeting, dentist, read the paper, sorted mail, listened to music, exercised, daydreamed, wrote a proposal, planned budget, grocery shopping, etc).*

➤ Then estimate as accurately as possible the time you spent on each activity in **Column 2**. Account for all 24 hours of the day.

☞ *You may want to suggest humorously that if participants end up with large blocks of time not accounted for, it may be a sign that they wasted a good share of the day simply spinning their wheels.*

2) The trainer outlines the following A-B-C time-use ranking system. As he describes each category, the trainer asks the group for examples of activities from their lists that fit that priority.

● **A's** are those tasks and activities that are related to your **major priorities** and are connected to your life goals.

● **B's are the tasks that must be done, but do not seem to be life-goal related**. Every day we complete tasks which must be done in order to give us the opportunity to move toward life goals (eg, making a living—"B", in order to provide for your family—"A").

● **C's are the activities that add very little if anything to one's life**. Like junk mail, these time-wasters clutter up our existence and quickly eat up our days.

3) Participants apply the A-B-C time rank system to their Time Log and calculate their "A" task percentage.

➤ Rate each activity you did yesterday as an "A," a "B" or a "C." Record your priorities in **Column 3**.

☞ *Allow plenty of time for people to make these judgments before moving on to the next step.*

➤ In **Column 4**, list all of yesterday's "A" activities and add up the total number of hours you spent on "A's."

➤ Divide this number by 24 to compute the percentage of time spent on "A's."

4) Participants then respond to the first three questions on the lower half of the worksheet, writing their answers on the back or on a blank sheet of paper.

B. The Skill of Using the ABC's (10–20 minutes)

5) The trainer shares guidelines for using the ABC's of time management, including some or all of the following points:

- Every day, no matter how "busy" or tired, make sure you spend at least five minutes working directly on a life goal. **Build in time for your "A's"—EVERY DAY!** Plan it into the schedule. If nothing happens in a day, nothing happens!

- Complete only as many "B's" as you must in order to give yourself the opportunity to keep working on your "A's."

- Every time a "C" comes into your life, throw it in a cardboard box. At the end of the month, throw the box in the garbage without even peeking. **Ignore the "C's."** If you mislabel a "C," it will come back at you as a "B" (eg, if you label your Mastercard bill a "C" priority one month, a call from the credit department will probably move it up to a "B" next month)!

- It's tempting to "click off" the "C's" rather than tackle the "A's" since "C's" are easy and quick to complete. Although this helps you feel like you've accomplished something, all you've really done is to stay busy! Spend time moving toward goals instead of just filling hours or crossing unimportant items off your list.

- Don't always work at other people's "A's" instead of your own.

- When you keep your priorities clearly in mind throughout the day, you *manage* your stress instead of letting it manage you.

- To make your time count, your life count, yourself count—spend yourself, your life and your time where it counts!

6) The trainer may read the **Each Day is a New Account** essay, as a challenge to the group.

7) The trainer invites participants to apply their insights about time priorities in a mini time-management plan.

   ➤ Drawing on what you've learned so far during this experience, answer *Questions 4* and *5* on your worksheet.

VARIATIONS

■ As part of *Step 7* participants form groups of three and compare insights about their time use patterns and resolutions for change. This is an ideal way for people to discover that everyone's priorities are different!

YESTERDAY'S TIME LOG ANALYSIS

Mentally think through the events of yesterday. List all the ways you spent your time yesterday (24 hours). Be as specific and accurate as possible. Use 1/4 hour segments. Be sure to total 24 hours!

Column 1 TASKS/ACTIVITIES	Column 2 TIME 1/4 hours	Column 3 PRIORITY A B C

Column 4 List all "A" Items	Time
TOTAL time spent on "A" items	

Percentage of time spent on "A" activities: _____ hours

(Divide TOTAL at left by 24)

1) Was yesterday typical? In what ways yes? In what ways no?

2) What do you applaud about your use of time yesterday? What do you deplore?

3) What would you like to do differently?

4) How could you put more "A" time into your day?

5) How will you start making that happen now?

EACH DAY IS A NEW ACCOUNT

If you had a bank that credited your account each morning with $86,000 . . .
That carried over no balance from day to day . . .
Allowed you to keep no cash in your accounts . . .
And every evening canceled
whatever part of the amount you had failed to use during the day . . .

What would you do?

Draw out every cent every day, of course, and use it to your advantage!

Well, you have such a bank . . . and its name is TIME.

Every morning, it credits you with 86,400 seconds.
Every night, it writes off as lost whatever of this you have failed to invest to good purpose.

It carries over no balances.
It allows no overdrafts.

Each day, it opens a new account with you.
Each night, it burns the records of the day.

If you fail to use the day's deposits, the loss is yours.

There is no going back.
There is no drawing against TOMORROW.

It is up to each of us to invest this precious fund of hours, minutes and seconds in order to get from it the utmost in health, happiness and success!

*From **The Stress Examiner** © Aid Association for Lutherans, 1982.*

Planning
& Closure

58 PERSONAL/PROFESSIONAL REVIEW

Participants review the session and affirm what they have gained from the learning experience.

GOALS

To promote application of concepts and transfer of learning to real life situations.

To end the session on a positive note.

GROUP SIZE

Unlimited; if the group is larger than 20, divide into small groups of 6–12 persons.

TIME FRAME

10–15 minutes

PROCESS

☞ *This exercise is most effective at the end of a session or workshop where* **Personal /Professional** *(p 2) is used.*

1) The trainer invites participants to reflect on the topics and activities of the day or session. She asks them to make a mental list of what they have learned about stress and coping, and about themselves.

2) Participants take turns sharing their responses to the following sentence stems:

➤ One thing I gained *personally* from this session.

➤ One thing I gained *professionally* (or for my work setting).

☞ *With more than 20 participants, divide into smaller groups (6–12 persons) for* **Step 2.**

3) The trainer summarizes the variety of learnings expressed and highlights any important issues that were not mentioned.

VARIATION

■ The trainer may want to enhance the transfer value by asking participants to state one specific application for each learning they identify.

©1994 Whole Person Press 210 W Michigan Duluth MN 55802   (800) 247-6789

59 MANAGER OF THE YEAR

In this closing affirmation participants write recommendations for themselves and campaign for *Stress Manager of the Year* awards.

GOALS

To enhance self-perceptions of competence for dealing with stress.

To provide closure for the learning experience.

To promote positive feedback among participants.

GROUP SIZE

Works best with 12–25 people.

TIME FRAME

45–60 minutes, depending on group size and creativity.

MATERIALS

Blank paper or **Nomination Memo** worksheets for everyone. **Campaign Guidelines** for each small group. A **Campaign Kit** for each group—a large bag filled with arts and crafts supplies such as newsprint, balloons, posterboard, crepe paper, blank buttons or name tags, string, straws, notecards, paper cups and plates, tape, glue, scissors, magic markers, etc. **Stress Manager of the Year** certificates for all.

PROCESS

☞ *This exercise is more fun if there is plenty of time for the creative campaign activities suggested. Although more "sophisticated" groups may initially resist such "childish" projects, most people eventually get caught up in the flow and find the process quite energizing and enlightening.*

1) The trainer distributes **Nomination Memo** worksheets and announces that every participant is a candidate for the *Stress Manager of the Year Award.*

➤ Write a memo of recommendation for yourself as *Stress Manager of the Year,* describing tough situations you have managed well, coping techniques you use often and/or skillfully, new strategies you have learned and practiced during this course.

☞ *Some people may balk at such blatant arrogance and self-aggrandizement. Reassure them that bragging this one time won't ruin their credibility or compromise their humility. Public affirmation of successful coping experiences is a powerful reinforcer and motivator for positive stress management in the future.*

2) If small sharing groups have been utilized during the learning experience, the trainer instructs participants to rejoin the most recent group. If not, participants are directed to form 3-person groups for this segment of the exercise. (10–15 minutes)

The trainer gives directions for sharing the *Memos*.

➤ Each person in turn should read your *Memo of Recommendation* to the others in your group.

➤ After each person reads, the others should add their positive comments to the *Recommendation*, noting how they have observed him coping well with stress—inside or outside of class.

➤ When you give someone feedback, record your comments on his *Memo* in the form of a P.S. and sign it.

➤ You will have about 10 minutes to share together, so take your time— but make sure everyone gets an opportunity for commendation.

3) When all group members have completed their turns, a representative is sent to the trainer who gives her a copy of the **Campaign Guidelines** and a **Campaign Kit**. The group plans a campaign for themselves as *Stress Managers of the Year*—following the guidelines—and uses the art materials to prepare a "floor demonstration" for the rally. (30 minutes)

4) The trainer reconvenes the group and sets the stage for a campaign rally. Each "delegation" is invited to take the floor for a brief "demonstration," parading their campaign creations, singing their song, shouting their slogans. The audience is encouraged to respond with enthusiastic applause, cheers and flag waving.

5) The trainer distributes a certificate suitable for framing to each participant designating her as *Stress Manager of the Year*.

VARIATION

■ If group members know each other well, they could draw names or choose partners and write memos of recommendation for each other instead of for themselves.

NOMINATION MEMO

TO: Selection Committee

RE: Stress Manager of the Year Award Nomination for:

_____
name

MY LETTER OF RECOMMENDATION:

_____
_____
_____
_____
_____
_____
_____
_____
_____
_____
_____
_____
_____
_____
_____
_____
_____
_____
_____
_____
_____
_____
_____
_____
_____
_____
_____
_____
_____
_____

CAMPAIGN GUIDELINES

You have 30 minutes to devise a campaign for this group as *Stress Managers of the Year*. Make sure that everyone is included in all parts of the campaign planning and preparation.

1) *Start by listing your common stressors and the coping strengths* the people in your group have demonstrated.

2) *Decide on a name* for yourselves that reflects your stress or affirms your management style (eg, "The Vegetarians," "The Parents of Adolescents," "The Type AB's," "The Support Staff Supporters").

3) *Brainstorm together a number of slogans* that describe your successful stress management styles or specific strategies you recommend for others (eg, "A mile a day keeps the blues away!" or "Eat, drink and be merry—in moderation only," or "Ban the butts," or "Work groups who play together stay together").

4) *Make up a theme song* for yourselves, if you have time.

5) *Use the supplies in your Campaign Kit* to make posters, balloons, placards, symbols, banners, awards, mementos, hats, badges, or any other props for use in promoting your group at the *Managers of the Year Rally*. Have fun! Be wild, zany and creative! Most of all, be affirming of each other and your accomplishments.

60 GOALS, OBSTACLES, ACTIONS

This in-depth planning exercise helps participants set goals, formulate strategies for moving toward their goals, and monitor their progress.

GOALS

To help participants identify a limited number of specific behavior change goals.

To formulate a plan of action for overcoming the obstacles that hold them back, and to monitor their step-by-step progress toward their goals.

GROUP SIZE

Unlimited; also effective in work with individuals.

TIME FRAME

30–60 minutes

MATERIALS

Blank paper and two or three **Goals, Obstacles, Actions** worksheets for each person.

PROCESS

A. Formulating the Goals (15–30 minutes)

1) The trainer distributes two sheets of blank paper for goal setting.

   ➤ Write down a list of personal goals related to the course/workshop. Record as many ideas as you like.

   ☞ *Use whatever warm-up seems appropriate, based on the style and content of the course. You may want to review the subjects covered and ask participants to peruse their own notes. Or if participants have kept a running "wish list" (see **Wellness 2**, p 52), have them refer to this list as they begin selecting their goals.*

2) The trainer asks participants to reflect on their initial list of goals based on the following criteria.

   ☞ *Be sure to give participants enough time between questions to register their responses.*

➤ Are these your own goals, or are they expectations someone else has set for you? Cross out those that are not fully your own.

➤ Are the goals realistic and attainable? Cross out those that you believe are impossible for you now.

➤ Are they stated positively? ("I want to quit smoking" is stated negatively. The positive goal is "I want to be a non-smoker!") Rephrase your goals into positive statements of intention.

➤ Are you willing to begin working right now to achieve these goals? Cross out all those to which you respond "no." Hold them for some later date.

3) The trainer asks participants to select 1–3 goals for further in-depth work, and to list those goals selected on a second sheet of paper.

☞ *For this exercise the maximum number of goals should be three— one or two would be preferable.*

4) The trainer asks participants to refine their goals by responding to the following issues:

☞ *Give participants enough time between questions to register their responses.*

➤ Make each general goal very specific—what, when, where. ("I want to be happier" is a goal, but it's not specific. "To be happier, I want to improve my relationship with Bob" is specific.)

➤ Check whether the specific wants are consistent with your belief system—your values, self-concept, long-range goals, commitments, etc. If not, modify the goal or cross it off your list.

➤ For each specific goal answer the following questions:
  ➣ What might I have to give up in order to reach this goal?
  ➣ Am I willing to give this up?
     What parts of this goal don't I want to touch right now?
     What moves might I be willing to make now?

B. Confronting the Barriers (5–15 minutes)

5) The trainer distributes one or more **Goals, Obstacles, Actions** worksheets with instructions.

➤ Write one of your specific goals in the upper left-hand corner of the worksheet.

➤ List all the roadblocks and obstacles that have kept you from reaching this goal in the past. Answer the questions in *Column 1*, *Obstacles and Roadblocks.*

Why have you not already achieved this?
What's stopping you?

➤ Write as many responses as you can.

➤ Now list possible solutions for overcoming each separate obstacle and record these ideas in *Column 2, Possible Solutions.*

☞ *If participants are working on more than one goal, be sure they use a different worksheet for each one and complete* **Step 5** *for each separate goal before moving on to* **Part C**.

C. Formulating the Action Plan (5–15 minutes)

6) The trainer invites participants to consider how they might implement some of their potential solutions.

➤ Look over your list in *Column 2* and circle all the activities you will undertake in order to remove each barrier and move toward your goal(s).

➤ Then decide on the specific timing for each activity to which you are committing yourself. (What will you do? When? Where? How often? For how long?) Record this information in *Column 3, Timing.*

7) The trainer challenges participants to identify a reward they will experience or give themselves when they have successfully completed each activity. These are recorded in *Column 4, Rewards.*

8) To clarify their action plan, participants complete the sentence stems at the bottom of the worksheet.

☞ *Participants complete* **Steps 6–8** *for each goal.*

D. Monitoring the Progress (5–10 minutes)

9) The trainer challenges participants to set up a system for evaluating their progress towards their goals.

➤ Set specific appointments (daily, weekly, monthly) with yourself for monitoring your performance and for evaluating the success of each activity.

➤ Get out your calendar right now and mark these dates.

Remind participants to reward themselves for following through on their plans, even if the goal is not reached. After all, the plan was only an "estimate" of what might help them achieve the goal. However, participants are not to reward themselves for planned activities they never complete—even if the goal was reached.

10) The trainer concludes with a reinforcing homework assignment.

➤ When evaluating your progress at the appointed time(s), mark down dates when activities were accomplished, revise plans as necessary for unfinished goals, set new goals and begin again.

➤ Record their progress in *Column 5* of the worksheet or in a separate journal.

 After the initial weekly or monthly checkpoints are completed, participants are to continue to replan at least once each year, and to reward themselves for whatever positive change they have maintained. They may want to select a special day such as their birthday, anniversary or New Year's Eve for this yearly checkup.

It is important for future reference that participants track all progress in writing, and record the results of these "performance checks" in a log book of their choosing.

*Inform participants that if they temporarily go off course, they are not failures! Encourage people to re-examine their goals. If they no longer desire the goal, drop it! If they are still intent on reaching it, they should analyze what went haywire, learn from the difficulty they've faced and formulate a new plan of action—**in writing!***

GOALS, OBSTACLES, ACTIONS

My goal: _____

(1) OBSTACLES AND ROADBLOCKS	(2) POSSIBLE SOLUTIONS AND ACTIVITIES PLAN OUTLINE
Why have I not already achieved this? What's stopping me?	*How could I overcome these obstacles by using my strengths and resources?*
A	
B	
C	
A	
B	
C	
A	
B	
C	
A	
B	
C	
A	
B	
C	

As I reach toward this goal I will be/have more:

GOALS, OBSTACLES, ACTIONS

3) TIMING	4) REWARDS I WILL EXPERIENCE	5) TRACKING PROGRESS
By When? How many times? Time of day? Etc.	*Intrinsic benefits; self rewards*	*Completed by:*

Detailed comments and notes on my plan to reach this goal:

61 25 WORDS OR LESS

Participants exchange advice for managing stress.

GOALS

To help participants articulate what they have learned about stress management.

To add drama, suspense and energy to the transfer-of-learning process.

GROUP SIZE

Works best with 8–40 people.

TIME FRAME

10–15 minutes; more with larger groups

MATERIALS

3"x5" index cards for all participants.

For variations: Blank stamped postcards, magic markers, crayons, colored pencils, stickers, etc.

PROCESS

1) The trainer announces that participants have finally attained the status of stress management experts and will now have a chance to demonstrate their wisdom. He distributes a 3"x5" notecard to everyone with the following instructions:

   ➤ Please write down, in 25 words or less, your response to the question, "What is your best advice for managing stress?"

2) The trainer collects all the cards and mixes them up. One-by-one each participant is invited to choose a card and read out loud the "words to the wise" written on it.

3) Participants are encouraged to take their chosen advice card home, display it in a prominent place, read it as least once a day and heed whatever advice it gives.

VARIATIONS

■ Paragraphs of advice could be written on a postcard and decorated with drawings, doodles, designs or stickers. Each participant writes her name and address on her card. The trainer collects the cards and sends them to participants at a later date (one week, one month, six months) for posting on the refrigerator, mirror or bulletin board as a reminder.

■ The trainer (or someone in the group) could collect all advice cards, type up everyone's suggestions, duplicate the list and distribute it to all as a "Primer on Stress Management."

TRAINER'S NOTES

62 STRESS & COPING JOURNAL

This on-going homework assignment helps participants monitor their stress and apply the management techniques learned during a several week course.

GOALS

To facilitate application of concepts to real-life situations.

To monitor stress levels and progress in implementation of coping skills.

GROUP SIZE

Any size; a good tool for use with individuals as well.

TIME FRAME

5–10 minutes; three 15–30 homework periods.

MATERIALS

Copies of the **Stress and Coping Journal Format** for everyone; participants will also need to obtain their own journals or notebooks.

PROCESS

1) The trainer introduces the concept of a stress diary or journal as a useful tool for documenting stress-provoking situations, monitoring reactions and tracking the effectiveness of management strategies.

2) The trainer distributes **Stress and Coping Journal Formats**, commenting that each journal entry should be written narrative style and include responses to all three areas indicated on the format. Participants are directed to obtain a notebook and keep a journal for the next week (or whatever period between sessions). They are to write in the journal at least three times a week.

   ☞ *The trainer may read an excerpt from her own journal as an example, but will also want to underscore the reality that each person's style can and should be unique.*

3) The trainer collects the journals a day or two before the next class. She reviews the contents and then returns them to participants at the class. The journal is then used again for recording observations during the next week.

For maximum benefit to participants, the trainer should read each journal thoroughly and write comments that give feedback on stress and coping skills. Be generous with affirmation as people experiment with new behaviors.

TRAINER'S NOTES

Submitted by Mary O'Brien Sippel.

STRESS AND COPING JOURNAL FORMAT

This journal is a tool to help you record significant information about the stress in your life, your coping style and how you apply what you've learned in class to your life situations.

Be sure to write in your journal at least three times during the week.

Record objective specifics (dates, times, activities, etc) as well as your observations, thoughts, feelings, etc.

Write each entry on the same day that the experience you are describing occurred.

➤ Describe the day's experiences with special attention to any aspect of the day that was particularly stressful or exciting.

➤ Relate the topics discussed in the last class to the stress of this day.

➤ Recount the various coping skills you used during the day to manage this stress or to view it differently. Comment on the effectiveness of each strategy.

Group
Energizers

63 THE GARDEN

This poignant parable focuses on the difference between "play" and "scoring."

GOALS

To help participants reflect on the purpose of life, interactions with others and play.

TIME FRAME

5 minutes

PROCESS

1) The trainer reads the parable, *The Garden.*

2) The trainer asks participants to identify a specific instance when they turned "play" into the "scoring achievement syndrome" and a specific instance when they played "simply for the fun of it."

3) The trainer encourages participants to search out and treasure those moments when they are able to let down their guard, let go of responsibility and turn off the scoreboard in their heads (eg, family reunion, holding an infant, laughing with others, watching a parade, etc).

VARIATION

■ This reading serves as a wonderful warm-up for *The Month of Fundays* (p 61).

The author of this story is Ann Herbert—or so our dog-eared copy says. Someone gave it to us years ago with no reference by Ann's name. In work- shops across the country we've asked, "Who and where is Ann Herbert?" but so far no one has known. It's a beautiful parable that has touched many. Will the real Ann Herbert please stand up?

THE GARDEN Reading

In the beginning, God didn't make just two people, he made a bunch of us. Because he wanted us to have a lot of fun, and he said you can't really have fun unless there's a whole gang of you. He put us in Eden which was a combination garden and playground and park and told us to have fun.

At first we did have fun just like he expected. We rolled down the hills, waded in the streams, climbed on the trees, swung on the vines, ran in the meadows, frolicked in the woods, hid in the forest, and acted silly. We laughed a lot.

Then one day this snake told us that we weren't having real fun because we weren't keeping score. Back then, we didn't know what score was. When he explained it, we still couldn't see the fun. But he said we should give an apple to the person who was best at all the games and we'd never know who was best without keeping score. We could all see the fun of that, of course, because we were all sure we were best.

It was different after that. We yelled a lot. We had to make up new scoring rules for most of the games. Others, like frolicking, we stopped playing because they were too hard to score.

By the time God found out what had happened we were spending about 45 minutes a day actually playing and the rest of the time working out scoring. God was wroth about that—very, very wroth. He said we couldn't use his garden anymore because we weren't having fun. We told him we were having lots of fun. He was just being narrow minded because it wasn't exactly the kind of fun he originally thought of.

He wouldn't listen.

He kicked us out, and he said we couldn't come back until we stopped keeping score. To rub it in (to get our attention, he said), he told us we were all going to die and our scores wouldn't mean anything anyway.

He was wrong. My cumulative, all-game score now is 16,548 and that means a lot to me. If I can raise it to 20,000 before I die, I'll know I've accomplished something. Even if I can't, my life has a great deal of meaning because I've taught my children to score high and they'll be able to reach 20,000 or even 30,000.

Really, it was life in the garden that didn't mean anything. Fun is great in its place but without scoring there's no reason for it. God actually has a very superficial view of life and I'm certainly glad my children are being raised away from his influence. We were lucky. We're all very grateful to the snake.

By Ann Herbert

64 HAND-TO-HAND CONTACT

In this soothing relaxation break participants trade hand massages. This technique is especially effective for people who use their fingers and hands for extended periods or those who experience chronic discomfort in these areas.

GOALS

To reduce tension in fingers and hands.

To provide a non-threatening experience that facilitates the learning of a massage procedure.

GROUP SIZE

Unlimited.

TIME FRAME

10 minutes

MATERIALS

Hand Massage handout.

PROCESS

1) The trainer introduces this energizer by describing briefly the effect of finger and hand tension on the total body. The trainer points out that massage is an ideal technique for reducing some of that tension—by helping muscles relax and stimulating increased blood supply to the area.

2) The trainer asks participants to pair up with a neighbor for a refreshing relaxation break. She distributes **Hand Massage** handouts and participants follow along as she describes the process of hand massage.

   ☞ *You may want to demonstrate the process with a volunteer. Be sure to show all the different kinds of strokes that are used (eg, thumb circles, subtle back and forth motions with fingertips, long sweeps, gentle pulling on fingers, kneading, etc). Encourage participants to practice on their own hands, experimenting with a variety of strokes and pressures.*

3) Partners decide who will be the first receiver. The trainer talks the whole group slowly through the massage, using the instructions on the handout. The process is repeated on the other hand, with the trainer directing the pace.

☞ *Overhead projection of the hand massage diagram provides a hands-free ready reference for the masseur.*

4) Partners switch roles and repeat *Step 3.*

5) The trainer may ask for comments and observations. She reminds participants that self-massage is a relaxation technique they can use whenever and wherever they need tension relief—finding a friend to exchange with doubles the benefits!

VARIATION

■ This exercise can be taught as a "do-it-yourself" process, rather than a shared experience.

TRAINER'S NOTES

Genie L Wessel submitted this routine which is based on a hand massage technique she leaned from John Davis at the University of Maryland.

HAND MASSAGE

RECEIVER:

1) Begin by warming and increasing the electric field between your hands. Slowly rub your palms together for 1-2 minutes.

GIVER:

2) Take one of the receiver's hands between your two hands; hold it gently.
3) Circle the wrist with both your hands; hold for 60 seconds.
4) Move slowly from wrist to the tip of the thumb, massaging gently. Repeat on all fingers, following the diagram.

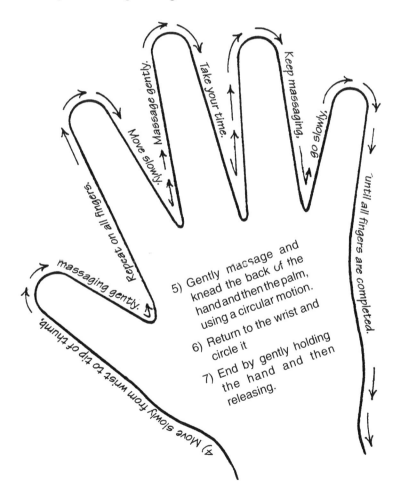

5) Gently massage and knead the back of the hand and then the palm, using a circular motion.

6) Return to the wrist and circle it

7) End by gently holding the hand and then releasing.

©1994 Whole Person Press 210 W Michigan Duluth MN 55802   (800) 247-6789

65 HELPERS ANONYMOUS

In this tongue-in-cheek initiation rite, participants confess their addiction to helping and learn the H.A. theme song.

GOALS

To encourage participants to laugh at a stress-producing habit.

To remind participants that their wants and needs are important.

GROUP SIZE

Works best with 20 or more people.

TIME FRAME

5 minutes

MATERIALS

Newsprint, transparency or handout with the **Helpers Anonymous Theme Song** lyrics.

PROCESS

☞ *This exercise is a perfect companion to **Hooked on Helping** (p 36).*

1) The trainer introduces the exercise by welcoming all the new members of Helpers Anonymous to this initiation meeting. He congratulates them for taking this important step on the road to conquering their addiction to helping and invites them to take the next important step— confession.

2) Participants are instructed to stand, turn to the person on their left and introduce themselves, using the phrase, "I'm (first name) and I'm hooked on helping."

    ☞ *The trainer will probably want to liven up this step to help people overcome their resistance. Suggest hand on heart while confessing. Remind the group that the Helpers Anonymous acronym— HA—encourages laughter as essential to recovery.*

3) The trainer teaches the **Helpers Anonymous Theme Song** to the group, using newsprint, overhead or handouts for the lyrics. The group sings the song once in unison complete with the actions indicated.

☞ *The trainer will need to help people get into the swing of things by dramatically modeling the pointing actions and encouraging the group to exaggerate their motions.*

4) After everyone has learned the theme song, the trainer divides the group into four sections for singing in rounds. The sections sing the song through 3 times, singing the 3 first lines more softly each time and the last 3 lines more loudly. The last time through, the groups whisper the first lines and shout the last one!

HELPERS ANONYMOUS Theme Song

Tune: "Frere Jacques"

Hooked on helping, hooked on helping!
Care for you! (point to someone)
And you, too! (point to someone else)

No more one-way giving, (wag finger)
Time for healthy living! (point to watch)
I count, too! I count, too! (point to self)

Original lyrics by Nancy Loving Tubesing.

©1994 Whole Person Press 210 W Michigan Duluth MN 55802   (800) 247-6789

66 MUSICAL MOVEMENT

A montage of musical styles provides the background and beat for tension-reducing interpretive movement.

GOALS

To expand awareness of the value of music and movement as coping techniques.

To provide a playful interlude.

GROUP SIZE

Unlimited, as long as the space is adequate.

TIME FRAME

10–15 minutes; can easily be expanded.

MATERIALS

Record or cassette player with various instrumental recordings.

PROCESS

1) The trainer introduces this exercise with a few comments on the power of music to evoke a variety of moods and feelings.

   ● The combination of music and body movement can be energizing or relaxing or both.

2) Participants are invited to stand and spread themselves around the room so everyone has space to move freely. The trainer gives instructions for the movement activity.

   ➤ Close your eyes, take a few deep breaths, let your mind clear and tune in to your body.

   ☞ *After a moment or two of silent concentration, turn on the music. Start with an irresistible tune and beat such as a Sousa march, William Tell Overture, Kay Gardner, Tiajuana Brass, Star Wars, Chariots of Fire, Strauss Waltz or a current rock hit.*

   ➤ Listen closely, allowing the music to flow into your body.

➤ Start moving with the music. Keep your eyes closed, and let your body move naturally with the music.

➤ As you continue to move, allow your body to interpret the music by swaying, rocking, marching, dancing, stretching, spinning—whatever the beat prompts you to do.

☞ *Some people may need extra encouragement to loosen up and enjoy this exercise. The trainer could suggest specific movements to try (clap, snap fingers, tap feet, skip, twist and turn, wave arms, etc). Remind the group to hear the beat and let their bodies keep time.*

3) *Step 2* is repeated several times, each time using a different musical selection (slow, fast, loud, soft, jazz, classical, folk, etc).

VARIATIONS

■ One person can lead the group in follow-the-leader interpretive movements.

■ Participants pair up and interpret the first musical selection together. For the second selection, two dyads join together and move to the music as quartets. Two quartets join and work together as a group of eight to interpret the next selection. This doubling process is continued until the entire group is involved in a giant communal dance.

TRAINER'S NOTES

67 ROUND OF APPLAUSE

In this hand-warming and heart-warming energizer participants applaud their accomplishments and give each other a standing ovation.

GOALS

To promote affirmation as a stress management strategy.

To boost group energy.

TIME FRAME

2 minutes

PROCESS

☞ *This exercise has a powerful impact when repeated several times during a workshop or session.*

1) The trainer asks the group to warm up their hands by applauding something or someone they are grateful for (eg, conference organizing committee, the cooks, a winning football team, an approaching holiday, what they've learned in the course, their family or friends, etc).

   ☞ *In this first round, the trainer should either specify the target of appreciation or ask for suggestions from the group and choose one.*

2) The trainer asks people to think of another target for their appreciation and once again provide a round of applause. As the clapping gains momentum, the trainer leads the group into a standing ovation, exhorting participants to whistle, cheer, stamp and shout with reckless abandon!

VARIATION

■ In *Step 2*, participants could request a standing ovation for themselves or nominate someone else in the group for a heart-warming experience. In either case, the person making the suggestion should state why the recipient needs or deserves the applause.

---

68 SEAWEED AND OAK

Participants alter their energy flow, using fantasy to become as flexible as floating seaweed and as sturdy as an oak tree.

GOALS

To become aware of how thoughts and energy flow are interrelated.

To compare spontaneity and control in two contrasting experiences of relaxation.

TIME FRAME

5–10 minutes

MATERIALS

Seaweed and Oak instructions.

PROCESS

1) The trainer introduces the exercise, inviting participants to join him in experiencing two types of mind and body relaxation. He reads the **Seaweed and Oak** instructions.

2) The trainer facilitates a group discussion regarding situations when spontaneity and control are most appropriate, asking questions like:

    ✔ When is it more appropriate to be spontaneous and flexible like the seaweed (eg, on your birthday, running in the park, relaxing with friends, playing with the kids, etc)?

    ✔ When is it more appropriate to be strong and controlled like the oak (eg, before an exam or job interview, during a confrontation, performance, etc)?

VARIATION

■ This exercise can be done in dyads. One person stands behind the other. The person in front closes her eyes and follows the instructions as read by the trainer (or her partner). The person behind plays the ocean (for the seaweed) and the wind (for the oak tree) gently pushing his partner's shoulders from side to side to test her energy flow and heighten her awareness of her responses.

Submitted by Martha Belknap.

©1994 Whole Person Press 210 W Michigan Duluth MN 55802   (800) 247-6789

SEAWEED AND OAK Script

Stand comfortably with arms relaxed at your sides, knees unlocked, eyes closed.

> *Slowly shift your weight from side to side.*

Think about a piece of seaweed, *firmly attached to the ocean floor but free to move gently with the movement of the water.*

> *Focus your attention **above your head** and imagine becoming that piece of seaweed.*

> *You are drifting, floating, moving easily and freely, changing form with the tide and the current, feeling light and **relaxed.***

Come back to the center position and open your eyes.

> *Then close your eyes again.*

Think about a strong oak tree *in the forest with firm roots growing deep into the earth.*

> *Focus your attention **into your abdomen** and imagine becoming that oak tree.*

> *Feel your roots growing down your legs, out through the bottom of your feet into the ground. Feel a strong connection with the earth beneath you.*

> *You are strong and sturdy and secure. Although the wind may move your branches, you are very safe in a storm.*

> *You are grounded and centered, feeling your inner strength, feeling firm and **relaxed.***

69 STRESS STRETCHERS

This quick energizer uses rubberbands to illustrate the tension/relaxation dynamics of stress and to demonstrate the need for creativity in coping.

GOALS

To illustrate the individuality of healthy stress and tension levels.

To get the creative juices flowing and prepare participants for expanding their coping skill repertoire.

To laugh, have fun and relieve the tension of talking about stress.

GROUP SIZE

Unlimited; 20–35 works well.

TIME FRAME

5–10 minutes maximum; keep the pace moving.

MATERIALS

Bags of rubberbands—mixed colors and sizes.

PROCESS

☞ *This exercise makes an excellent transition from a stress identification/assessment process to a coping skills presentation.*

1) The trainer sets a light, playful mood while she introduces the exercise as a transition from stress identification to coping strategies. She passes the bag of rubberbands around the group, telling each person to take one.

2) Participants are invited to explore and comment on the effect of tension on their rubberbands. The trainer guides the process and asks facilitative questions:

   ✔ Stretch the rubberband, what happens? (eg, gets thin, gets tight, might break, etc)

   ✔ Relax the tension, what happens? (eg, nothing, snaps back, gets floppy, etc)

   ➤ Put it between your teeth and pull on the other end. Find the right balance of stretch so that it makes pleasing music. Twang away.

The trainer comments on the similarity between people and rubber-bands—with just the right amount of tension, we make beautiful music!

3) The trainer asks participants to brainstorm all the uses of a rubberband (eg, make music, chew it to relieve tension, use as slingshot to keep people away, organize things together, repair broken toy, as a reminder around the wrist, to decorate, to tie up hair, etc).

The trainer points out the similarity of the rubberband to effective stress management skills (eg, need to be flexible, need to have multiple uses, need to be creative, skills need to change with situations, need at times to stretch and grow, etc).

4) The trainer praises participants for their creativity and suggests that they will find the same success in designing their own stress management program.

5) The trainer recommends that people keep their rubberbands in pocket or purse (or around their wrists) as a cue to remind them of something they learned during this session (eg, "When I see my rubberband, I'll take a deep breath," or "When I notice my rubberband, I'll remind myself to be flexible," etc).

TRAINER'S NOTES

Submitted by Sally Strosahl.

70 TARGET PRACTICE

Participants choose a coping skill and experiment with using it during a coffee or lunch break.

GOALS

To visualize where, when and how a specific stress management strategy might be useful.

To practice a new or under-utilized coping skill.

TIME FRAME

10 minutes

PROCESS

☞ *This exercise works best just before a scheduled break and when preceded by a coping skills assessment, such as **Pileup Copers** (p 54), **The AAAbc's of Stress Management** (Stress 1, p 49) or **Coping Skills Assessment** (Stress 1, p 63).*

1) The trainer invites participants to join in a stress management experiment. She asks each person to pick a coping skill he would like to develop more fully (eg, assertiveness, contact, positive self-talk, humor, surrender, play, exercise, value clarification, listening, etc). Participants write down the target skill.

2) The trainer asks participants two questions about implementing this skill, allowing plenty of time for people to silently imagine their responses:

   ➤ Concentrate on the skill you would like to improve. Imagine how you would act using that skill effectively to manage some of the stress in your life. Where would you especially like to try it? When? Picture yourself using the skill expertly in a stressful situation.

   ➤ Now, I'd like you to imagine how you would act here at this workshop/class if you were using this skill effectively. How could this skill be implemented right here and now?

3) The trainer announces a coffee break and challenges participants to practice their target skills. They are to use that skill and that skill only during the entire break time, acting as if they were already proficient and comfortable with the technique.

©1994 Whole Person Press 210 W Michigan Duluth MN 55802   (800) 247-6789

4) After the break, the trainer invites reports from participants on what they experienced during this practice session.

TRAINER'S NOTES

71 TEN-SECOND BREAK

Participants learn a ten-second breathing and auto-suggestion break that's ideal for instant stress relief.

GOALS

To interrupt or prevent tension build-up.

TIME FRAME

5 minutes

MATERIALS

Ten-Second Break handouts for everyone.

PROCESS

1) The trainer solicits from the group examples of stressful situations when they would like a reliable "instant" stress relief technique (eg, before exams, during arguments, when irritated, when hassled, when anxious, etc).

2) The trainer distributes the **Ten-Second Break** handouts and informs participants that this simple exercise can be a lifesaver for stressful situations. He describes and demonstrates the technique following the instructions on top of the handout and then leads the group through several practice routines.

   The trainer points out that if time does not permit a full *Ten-Second Break, Step 3* alone is often an effective stopgap measure.

3) Participants are encouraged to try this *Ten-Second Break* whenever they are irritated—no matter how small an irritation. It also can give them "breathing room" in conflict situations where they are trying to decide what to do or how to act.

4) The trainer points out that a frequent source of stress for many people is the telephone. He teaches the group the modified *Ten-Second Break* sequence for phone calls as described on the handout.

©1994 Whole Person Press 210 W Michigan Duluth MN 55802   (800) 247-6789

10-SECOND BREAK

BASIC ROUTINE

STEP 1

Smile as you think to yourself
"My body doesn't need this _____."

(irritation or stress)

STEP 2

Take a slow, deep **belly breath**—
Count to 4 slowly on the inhale and on the exhale.

STEP 3

Take a second deep belly breath—
Close your eyes at the top of the inhalation.

As you exhale . . . imagine (visualize or feel) something warm entering your body at your head . . . and flowing down into your hands and feet.

*Heaviness and warmth are flowing in. Think the phrase,"**I am calm.**"*

STEP 4

Open your eyes.

MODIFIED ROUTINE FOR PHONE CALLS

STEP A

When the phone **begins to ring:**
Do **STEP 3** (above) first—then answer the phone.

STEP B

DURING the phone call:
Relax your shoulders and jaw.
Breathe from your abdomen as rhythmically as possible.

STEP C

AFTER the phone call:
Do the complete **Ten-Second Break, STEPS 1 - 4.**

---

72 TREASURE CHEST

In this colorful guided fantasy participants discover a treasure chest containing a "gift" they need.

GOALS

To synthesize and "own" what has been learned during the session.

GROUP SIZE

Unlimited.

TIME FRAME

15–20 minutes

MATERIALS

Treasure Chest Fantasy script.

PROCESS

1) The trainer invites participants to experience a guided fantasy that will provide a relaxing wrap-up to any segment of a session or course. She reads the **Treasure Chest Fantasy** script, customizing the instructions to fit the group situation and course content to be highlighted.

   ☞ *Before beginning the fantasy, the trainer will need to decide what "gift" she wants participants to discover in the treasure chest. The "gift" could be related to the overall goals of the course (eg, the gift of what you need to manage your stress better) or it could be tied to the specific topic of this session (eg, the gift of relaxation or assertiveness or a positive outlook, etc).*

2) Participants pair up and describe the "gifts" they discovered. (5 minutes)

Submitted by Krysta Eryn Kavenaugh.

TREASURE CHEST FANTASY Script

Put your feet flat on the floor . . . scoot your seat against the back of the chair . . . place your hands comfortably in your lap.

Take a deep breath . . . let it go . . . take another deep breath . . . let it go . . . take another deep breath . . . Close your eyes . . . Let your body relax . . . allow yourself to breathe deeply and heavily . . . as you inhale, inhale relaxation . . . as you exhale, exhale tension . . . Allow yourself to be calm and relaxed.

Now imagine yourself in a field of red . . . run through the field of red . . . see the poppies . . . see the cardinals . . . Allow yourself to experience red.

☞ *Let people experience "red" for about 45 seconds.*

Then go into a field of orange . . . allow yourself to experience orange . . . see the oranges . . . see the orange flowers . . . Allow yourself the experience of the field of orange . . . allow yourself to smell it . . . What does it taste like?

☞ *Again wait for approximately 45 seconds.*

Now imagine yourself in a field of yellow. See the yellow flowers . . . see the daisies and daffodils . . . see the canaries . . . and anything else yellow . . . Totally experience yellow . . . What does it sound like? . . . What does it feel like? . . . Immerse yourself in yellow.

☞ *Wait 45 seconds.*

Then go into a field of green . . . experience the incredible number of shades of green . . . Let the green surround you . . . experience the field of green.

☞ *Wait 45 seconds.*

Imagine yourself in a field of blue, sky blue . . . allow yourself to relax in blue . . . see the blue flowers . . . breathe in the blueness . . . Experience what blue feels like.

☞ *Wait 45 seconds.*

Now imagine a field of dark blue, indigo . . . see the bluebirds . . . see the blueberries . . . surround yourself with that dark blue . . . Allow that dark blue to surround you . . . What does it taste like? . . . What does it smell like?

☞ *Wait 45 seconds.*

Then imagine yourself in a field of purple, deep royal purple . . . see the violets . . . see the other purple flowers . . . Let yourself experience the purple . . . what it feels like . . . what it sounds like . . . what it tastes like.

☞ *Wait 45 seconds.*

Now imagine that all the colors become one and turn into a white light surrounding you . . . let the white light penetrate and envelope you.

Now you notice you're on a path in a forest . . . allow yourself to walk through the forest . . . until you become aware that you're coming to a clearing . . . There's a pond in the clearing . . . by the pond is your favorite tree . . . Let yourself sit by the tree . . . and think about   (the topic)   .

☞ *Insert a topic relevant to the course such as stress, relationships, humor, worrying, grief, health, coping.*

The pond is clear and deep . . . you can see the bottom . . . and you notice a chest is at the bottom of the pond.

Now imagine yourself—even if you can't swim, it's okay, you're safe . . . just imagine yourself diving into the pond and bringing up the treasure chest . . . bring it back over to where you are by the tree.

In just a minute, I'll ask you to open the treasure chest . . . Inside there will be a gift regarding   (the chosen topic)   . . . The gift will be a word . . . or a picture . . . or a thought . . . or a presence . . . Don't try to make anything happen . . . just let it come to you . . . if you don't get something during this process . . . just let that be okay . . . it will come to you later on today . . . or in your sleep.

Now, open the box . . . and see what gift is inside . . . and let the gift talk to you . . . telling you what it is for and what it means.

☞ *Wait approximately 30 seconds.*

If you have any questions, ask the gift now.

☞ *Wait approximately 30 seconds.*

Now you have a choice . . . In just a minute, I'll ask you to do one of two things . . . You can either close the box and put it back in the water . . . or . . . you can put your hands out in front of you . . . and imagine the treasure chest shrinking . . . shrinking small enough to fit into your hands . . . Then imagine opening your heart . . . and putting the treasure chest inside your heart for safe-keeping . . . Do one of those right now.

☞ *Wait 30 seconds.*

Now, get up and start walking along the path . . . and count from 1 to 5 . . . when you get to 5, you'll be back in this room.

TRAINER'S NOTES

Resources

GUIDE TO THE RESOURCES SECTION

This resources section is intended to provide assistance for planning and preparation as you develop and expand your stress management training and consulting in various settings.

TIPS FOR TRAINERS p. 136

Suggestions for designing presentations and workshops using the exercises in **Structured Exercises in Stress Management Volume 2** to best advantage. Practical ideas for getting participants involved in the learning process.

EDITORS' CHOICE p. 138

Recommendations from the editors on their favorite exercises from **Stress 2** and especially appropriate processes for tackling job stress issues.

> Four****Star Exercises: The Best of **Stress 2** p. 138
> Especially for the Workplace p. 140

WINNING COMBINATIONS p. 141

Session outlines for presentations and workshops of varying lengths using exercises from **Stress 2** in combination. Plus notes on natural companion processes from other **Structured Exercises** volumes.

> One-Shot Stress and Coping Presentations (10–90 min)
> Workshop on Stress and Self-Esteem (90 min– 3 hours)
> Hooked on Helping Workshop for Care-givers (90 min– 3 hours)

ANNOTATED INDEXES to Stress 2 p. 143

Guides to specific content segments and group activities incorporated in exercises from **Stress 2**, identified by page reference, time frame, brief description, and comments on use.

> Index to CHALKTALKS p. 143
> Index to DEMONSTRATIONS p. 144
> Index to PHYSICAL ENERGIZERS p.145
> Index to MENTAL ENERGIZERS p. 146
> Index to RELAXATION ROUTINES p. 147

CONTRIBUTORS/EDITORS p. 149

Data on trainers who have shared their best process ideas in this volume. All are highly skilled educators and most provide in-house training, consultation, or workshops that may be valuable to you in planning comprehensive stress management programs. Many contributors are also established authors of well-respected materials on stress, wellness, and training issues.

WHOLE PERSON PUBLICATIONS p. 153

Descriptions of trainer-tested audio, video and print resources available from the stress and wellness specialists.

©1994 Whole Person Press 210 W Michigan Duluth MN 55802   (800) 247-6789

TIPS FOR TRAINERS

Designing Presentations and Workshops Using
Structured Exercises in Stress Management Volume 2

As you will notice in just a cursory glance through this handbook, we believe strongly in designing educational experiences that actively involve participants in the learning process. When you draw on the resources of the group in your presentations, you empower people.

For most trainers, giving up the "authority" implicit in the typical lecture format is a risky proposition. We trainers are often afraid that we won't be perceived as an "expert." So we lecture, entertain and keep the focus on ourselves. Yet, if your goal is truly to help people change, information is not enough. Praise from your audience is not enough. What really counts are the discoveries participants make about their own unhealthy patterns and the choices they make to manage their stress more effectively.

Certainly you have expertise to offer your audiences. But the greatest gift you can give is to tap into the wisdom and creativity of individuals and the group as a whole. Their knowledge base, experiences and insights will enrich and expand your expertise. Asking for significant input can also help you tune in to the specific needs of your participants and tailor your comments, examples and activities to meet them more precisely.

Your task is to appeal to people with different learning styles, using a wide variety of strategies to get them involved. In whole person learning, the questions are as important as the content. Don't be intimidated by the small number of stubborn rationalists who may sit with their arms crossed, waiting for the "right" answers in outline form. In stress management there are no right answers, no simple solutions, and no single path.

Several "projective" exercises where major content is provided by large or small group discussion are included in this volume. We hope you will stretch yourself and experiment with some of these:

   39 **Four Quadrant Questions** p. 9–12
   41 **Exclusive Interview** p. 14–16
   52 **Consultants Unlimited** p. 70–72
   58 **Personal/Professional Review** p. 97
   59 **Manager of the Year** p. 98–102
   61 **25 Words or Less** p. 108–109
   62 **Stress and Coping Journal** p. 110–112

Individual reflection processes provide another vehicle for provoking insights and for stimulating participation. The following exercises in this volume use "empty" worksheets that call on the individual's resources to generate examples, assessments, strategies, etc.

©1994 Whole Person Press 210 W Michigan Duluth MN 55802   (800) 247-6789

45 Back to the Drawing Board p. 32–35
47 Circuit Overload p. 46–48
50 Month of Fundays p. 61–63
51 The Worry Stopper p. 64–69

Don't worry. If lecturing is your thing, and content is your focus, you'll find plenty of chalktalk notes and content outlines in most exercises. But please do accept our invitation to experiment with participant empowerment by trusting your audience—get them involved!

EDITORS' CHOICE

Although all 36 exercises in this volume are practical, creative and time-tested, we must admit that we use some more often than others. When people call and ask us for suggestions about which exercises to incorporate into their workshop designs, we typically recommend some of our favorites—processes that have worked over and over again with many audiences, readings and activities that are guaranteed to charm a group. We call these our FOUR****STAR choices.

Four****Star Exercises	Page	Comments (Timing)
39 Four Quadrant Questions	p. 9–11	This two-part exercise draws on the resources of the group and is easy to adapt to your content. Always works well. (15–20 min, 10–15 min)
42 The Fourth Source of Stress	p. 17–24	Self-esteem is a key source of stress— and a potential coping tool. Effective checklist and self-discovery process. (45–60 min)
45 Back to the Drawing Board	p. 32–35	We use this right brain process periodically with our own staff to monitor stress levels and affirm coping efforts. It's a real winner! (50–75 min)
47 Circuit Overload	p. 46–48	Easy, graphic, dependable warm-up for any stress presentation. (15–20 min)
48 I've Got Rhythm	p. 49–53	This classic from the original **Stress Skills** workshop always produces new insights. (15–20 min)
51 The Worry Stopper	p. 64–69	Everyone can identify with this universal stressor and quickly master the worry-stopper model. (30–40 min)
53 Attitude Adjustment Hour	p. 73–76	One of our favorite techniques for demonstrating the role of perception in creating and relieving stress. Especially fun for a group that knows each other and can practice the technique together later. (25–35 min)
57 The ABC's of Time	p. 92–96	Time management is always a hot topic for stress courses. This process is based on Alan Lakein's **How to Get Control of Your Time and Your Life.** (40–50 min)

©1994 Whole Person Press 210 W Michigan Duluth MN 55802   (800) 247-6789

60 Goals, Obstacles, Actions   A thorough planning process geared
                             p. 102–107   toward behavioral change. (60 min)

63 The Garden   This parable on play is our most fre-
                             p. 113–114   quently requested reading. (5 min)

ESPECIALLY FOR THE WORKPLACE

Workplace Stress Exercise

Page Comments (Time)

37B Personal/Professional p.2 Companion exercises for articulating
58 Personal/Professional   goals evaluating outcomes for the learn-
    Review   p. 97 ing experience. (10–15 min each)

43 Burnout Index   Quick checklist of stress-related symp-
    p. 25–27 toms appropriate for the harried profes-
    sional. (10–15 min)

45 Back to the Drawing Board May be a bit risky for intact work groups
    p. 32–35 with a highly authoritarian power structure.
    Otherwise, a dynamite exercise for getting
    to the heart of work stress.
    (50–75 min)

46 Hooked on Helping   See WORKSHOP outline below.
    p. 36–45 (60–90 min)

52 Consultants Unlimited   "Consultant" teams devise strategies
    p. 70–72 for managing each other's stress.
    Works best with mixed groups from
    different settings. (30–40 min)

55 Affirmative Action Plan   This exercise began as Nancy's word
    p. 81–87 game and turned out to be a potent
    attitude-changing experience for managing
    the stress of difficult personalities at work.
    (40–50 min)

57 The ABC's of Time   Time management is a good intro to
    p. 81–87 stress in the workplace. (40–50 min)

59 Manager of the Year   Nice closing affirmation for an extended
    p. 98–101 course. (45–60 min)

67 Round of Applause   Positive feedback process for many
    p. 122 settings. (2 min)

©1994 Whole Person Press 210 W Michigan Duluth MN 55802   (800) 247-6789

WINNING COMBINATIONS

One-Shot Stress Management Presentation (10–90 min)

For a brief (10–20 min) presentation, use the process described in Exercise 47, **Circuit Overload** (p. 46) or a brief version of **The Worry Stopper**, Exercise 51 (p. 64).

For a longer time slot (30–50 min), try Exercise 42, **The Fourth Source of Stress**, p. 17 or Exercise 44, **Dragnet**, p. 28 (30–40 min). Use an appropriate icebreaker from Exercise 37, **Introductions 4** (p. 1) and add Exercise 39, **Four Quadrant Questions**, p. 9 (10 min) for closure.

For a memorable hour-long presentation, begin with **Circuit Overload**, Exercise 47, p. 46 (15–20 min). Then focus on personal management styles using Exercise 49, **Pileup Copers**, p. 54 (45–60 min).

Workshop on Stress and Self-Esteem (90 min–3 hrs)

Begin with Exercise 40, **Life Event Bingo**, p. 12 (20–30 min). This mixer based on Holmes and Rahe's Social Readjustment Rating Scale highlights life changes that may be stressful.

The major portion of the workshop focuses on four sources of stress: anticipated life events, unexpected life events, accumulated strains, and personal trait stress (self-esteem). Use Exercise 42, **The Fourth Source of Stress**, p. 17, expanding your presentation of the first three sources as described on p. 21. Then spend the major portion of time exploring self-esteem as a stress generator and stress reliever. (60 min)

For a longer session or workshop, incorporate an esteem-building skill-training component here. Use Exercise 54, **Speak Up!**, p. 77 (40–45 min) to focus on assertiveness skills, or try Exercise 55, **Affirmative Action Plan**, p. 55 (40–50 min), using oneself (rather than a co-worker) as the target.

Be sure to allow time for one of these affirming closures to the learning experience:

> 49 **PILEUP Copers**, p. 54 (60 min)
> 59 **Manager of the Year**, p. 98 (45–60 min)
> 72 **Treasure Chest**, p. 131 (15–20 min)

Hooked on Helping Workshop for Care Givers (90 min–3 hrs)

For years we conducted two-day workshops focused on the special stresses of the helping professions. The process described in Exercise 11, **Lifetrap 2: Hooked on Helping**, p. 36 (60–90 min) is the heart of that workshop. Even if your audience is not exclusively health care or social service personnel, nearly everyone can identify with the issues of over-extension on the job and/or in relationships.

To expand your presentation of this important stress issue, choose one or more of the following "natural companions" from **Stress 2**.

The icebreaker **Wave the Magic Wand**, p. 2 (2–4 min), may help helpers articulate their unrealistic expectations and hopes for a magical solution.

The format of Exercise 41, **Exclusive Interview**, p. 14, appeals to human service professionals—they usually have good interviewing skills and enjoy the self-discovery process (25–30 min). Good starting point—or recast the questions to use as a closing assessment.

Job burnout is a critical issue for helpers. Incorporate Exercise 43, **Burnout Index**, p. 25 (10–15 min), in your exploration of the addiction trap in **Part C**.

Exercise 45, **Back to the Drawing Board**, p. 32 (50–75 min), makes a great companion exercise for a longer workshop format.

Play is a natural remedy for over-stressed care-givers. Include Exercise 50, **Month of Fundays**, p. 61 (20–30 min), as a skill-builder.

Most helpers have difficulty saying NO and asking for what they need. Exercise 54, **Speak Up!**, p. 77 (40–45 min), is a perfect skill-building module for an extended learning experience.

Be sure to read Exercise 63, **The Garden**, p. 113 (5 min), sometime during your presentation. It's a perfect parable for the over-burdened.

Exercise 64, **Hand-to-Hand Contact**, p. 115 (10 min), allows participants to practice receiving as well as giving.

For a nice closing visualization try Exercise 72, **Treasure Chest**, p. 131 (10–15 min). Participants discover a "gift" they need.

If you have other volumes in the **Structured Exercises** series, you can add even more pizzazz to your workshop:

Try the checklist from Exercise 7, **Stress Symptom Inventory** (**Stress 1**, 10–40 min) as an introduction to **Hooked on Helping**. Should help people get in touch with the cost of caring.

The process in Exercise 122, **Obligation Overload** (**Stress 4**, 45 min) provides an effective skill session for the overburdened.

Don't miss Exercise 139, **Merry-Go-Round** (**Stress 4,** 5–15 min)—a rowdy demonstration of the stress of taking on too many burdens.

ANNOTATED INDEXES

Index to CHALKTALKS

42 Fourth Source of Stress   Four sources of stress: anticipated
                          p. 17   changes, unexpected life events, accu-
                                  mulated strain and personal attitudes/
                                  patterns.
                          p. 19   Self-esteem is the key to stress manage-
                                  ment.
                          p. 20   Eight strategies for improving self-esteem.

43 Burnout Index   p. 25   Job stress and burnout.

45 Back to the Drawing Board   Principles for surviving stress in the work-
                          p. 35   place.

46 Lifetrap 2:   p. 37–45   The care-giving addiction and the beliefs
Hooked on Helping   that drive it.
                          p. 42   Strategies for coping with the addiction to
                                  care-giving.

48 I've Got Rhythm   p. 49   Life rhythm and stress.
                          p. 50   Matching your stress management plans
                                  to your rhythm.

49 PILEUP Copers   p. 54   The need for variety in coping skills.
                          p. 55   Positive and negative copers.

50 Month of Fundays   p. 61   The importance of play in managing
                                  stress.

51 Worry Stopper   p. 66   Worry and stress: worry wisely.

53 Attitude Adjustment Hour   Role of perception in causing and manag-
                          p. 73   ing stress.

54 Speak Up!   p.77   Assertiveness and stress.

55 Affirmative Action Plan   Affirmation as a stress reducer: acknow-
                          p. 81–84   ledge, respond, encourage, appreciate,
                                  cultivate the attitude of gratitude.

56 Anchoring   p. 88   Stimulus-response model for relaxation
                                  training.

57 The ABC's of Time   p. 93   The A-B-C time-use ranking system.
                          p. 94   Implementing the ABC time management
                                  system.

Index to DEMONSTRATIONS

48 I've Got Rhythm   p. 50   Get in touch with your natural rhythm and
                                        discover the consequences of resisting it.
                                        (5 min)

67 Round of Applause   p. 122 Demonstrates the power of affirmation
                                        as a stress management strategy. (2 min)

68 Seaweed and Oak   p. 123 Experience control and spontaneous
                                        flow. (5–10 min)

69 Stress Stretchers   p. 125 Rubberbands illustrate the tension/relaxa-
                                        tion dynamic of stress and demonstrate
                                        the need for creative coping. (5–8 min)

70 Target Practice   p. 127 On the spot skill practice. (10 min)

©1994 Whole Person Press 210 W Michigan Duluth MN 55802   (800) 247-6789

Index to PHYSICAL ENERGIZERS

40 Life Event Bingo   p. 12 Participants mill around getting acquainted
                                     Can be used anytime during the session.
                                     (10–30 min)

50 Month of Fundays   p. 61 Group brainstorms playful activities and
                                     then indulges in one or more.
                                     (20–30 min)

64 Hand-to-Hand Contact   Soothing hand massage.
                               p. 115 (10 min)

66 Musical Movement   p. 121 Interpretive movement to different musical
                                     styles will really rev up the crowd.
                                     (10–15 min)

68 Seaweed and Oak   p. 123 A group movement exercise in grounding
                                     and flexibility. (5–10 min)

©1994 Whole Person Press 210 W Michigan Duluth MN 55802   (800) 247-6789

Index to MENTAL ENERGIZERS

37A Alphabet Copers   p. 1   In a large group, use this technique to
                                        quickly generate a creative list of copers.
                                        (2–3 min)

45 Back to the Drawing Board   Drawing the stressors and energizers in
                              p. 32   your environment helps you see them
                                        differently. (50–75 min)

50 Month of Fundays   p. 61 Participants create a calendar of playful
                                        activities for each day of the month. Could
                                        be adapted for developing a calendar of
                                        coping techniques, exercise options,
                                        affirmations, etc. (20–30 min)

53 Attitude Adjustment Hour   Practice altering your viewpoint by retell-
                              p. 73   ing the story of your day from different
                                        perspectives. (25–35 min)
                              p. 76   Hilarious **Accident Reports** reading high-
                                        lights differing perceptions. (3–5 min)

58 ABC's of Time   p. 96 **Each Day Is A New Account** reading
                                        provides an incisive commentary on the
                                        value of time. (2 min)

59 Manager of the Year   p. 98 Creative group affirmation process.
                                        (45–60 min)

63 The Garden   p. 113 This play-full reading always makes its
                                        point with power. (5 min)

72 Treasure Chest   p. 131 In this colorful guided fantasy participants
                                        discover a "gift" they need. (15–20 min)

Index to RELAXATION ROUTINES

56 Anchoring   p. 88   Pairs guide each other in relaxing visualizations and "anchor" the feelings for future recall. (30 min)

64 Hand-to-Hand Contact   p. 115   A soothing hand massage for one or two. (10 min)

66 Musical Movement   p. 120   Experiment with non-threatening, tension-relieving body movement. (10–15 min)

71 Ten-Second Break   p. 129   Breathing and auto-suggestion routine for instant stress relief. (5 min)

©1994 Whole Person Press 210 W Michigan Duluth MN 55802   (800) 247-6789

TRAINER'S NOTES

CONTRIBUTORS

Martha Belknap, MA. 1170 Dixon Road, Gold Hill, Boulder CO 80302. 303/ 447-9642. Marti is an educational consultant with a specialty in creative relaxation and stress management skills. She has 30 years of teaching experience at all levels. Marti offers relaxation workshops and creativity courses through schools, universities, hospitals and businesses. She is the author of **Taming Your Dragons**, a book and cassette tape of creative relaxation activities for home and school.

Thomas G Boman, PhD. Professor, Dept of Education, Univ of Minnesota–Duluth, Duluth MN 55812. 218/726-7157 (w), 218/724-2317 (h). Tom is a practicing educator, in-service trainer and program developer. His work with teachers at all levels of experience allows him ample opportunity to study the secrets of maintaining professional and personal vitality. PhD in Educational Psychology, MA in Curriculum and Instruction, BS in Chemistry.

Sandy Christian, MSW. Clinical Supervisor, Lutheran Social Services, Duluth Counseling Center, Duluth MN 55802. 218/726-4769 (w), 218/728-3916 (h). Sandy is a licensed marriage and family therapist and a licensed independent clinical social worker who has for 20 years avoided the high burnout rate of her profession by sprinkling a large dose of teaching and peer support networking into her busy life. She continues to balance the abiding eustress and occasional distress of being a parent, as well as a social worker.

Joel Goodman, EdD. Director, The HUMOR Project, 110 Spring Street, Saratoga Springs NY 12866. 518/587-8770. Joel is a popular speaker, consultant and seminar leader who has presented to over 500,000 corporate managers, health care leaders, educators, and other helping professionals throughout the U.S. and abroad. Author of 8 books, Joel publishes **Laughing Matters** magazine and HUMORosources mail order bookstore catalog, and sponsors the annual international conference on "The Positive Power of Humor and Creativity."

Krysta Eryn Kavenaugh, MA, CSP. 955 Lake Drive, St Paul MN 55120. 800/ 829-8437 (w) 612/725-6763 (h). Krysta is a speaker, trainer, and consultant. Her mission is to take people "into the heart of wisdom." She speaks with style, substance, and spirit. She is also the managing editor of **Marriage** magazine. Her favorite keynote topic is "Romancing Yourself: Taking Care of You is Taking Care of Business." She also speaks on proactive support teams, turning adversity to our advantage, ecology, and customized business topics.

Gloria Singer, ACSW. 43 Rivermoor Landing, 125 Main Street, New Market NH 03857-1640. 603/659-7530. Gloria's background as a social worker and educator are valuable assets in her position as Director of E.A.P. Services, resource management consultants in Salem NH. In that capacity she has enjoyed designing site-specific programs in stress management and wellness as well as training, counseling and group work with employees and their families.

©1994 Whole Person Press 210 W Michigan Duluth MN 55802   (800) 247-6789

Mary O'Brien Sippel, RN MS. Licensed Psychologist, 22 East St Andrews, Duluth MN 55803. 218/723-6130 (w) 218/724-5935 (h). Educated as a nurse, Mary has spent over 25 years working the field of community health and education. She has conducted seminars on stress management, burnout prevention, and wellness promotion throughout the U.S. She is currently a personal counselor and adjunct faculty member at the College of St Scholastica, Duluth MN. She is also working on **Wildflower Adventures**, a book on getting food and weight in a healthy perspective for children.

Sally Strosahl, MA. Marriage & Family Therapist, 116 S Westlawn, Aurora IL 60506. 708/897-9796. Sally has an MA in clinical psychology; trained at the Wholistic Health Center; researched the relationship between stress and illness. In addition to her private practice in marriage and family therapy, Sally frequently presents workshops in the areas of stress and wellness management, burnout prevention, body image and size acceptance, and marriage enrichment. She particularly enjoys working with "systems" (family, work groups, agencies, business, churches) to help enhance each member's growth and well-being.

David X Swenson, PhD. Assoc Professor of Management, College of St Scholastica, 1200 Kenwood Ave, Duluth MN 55811. 218/723-6476 (w) 218/724-6903 (h). A licensed consulting psychologist, Dave maintains a private practice in addition to his educational and therapeutic roles at the college. He provides consultation and training to human services, health and law enforcement agencies and is the author of **Stress Management in the Criminal Justice System**. Dave also develops stress management software.

Randy R Weigel, PhD. Associate Professor, Dept of Home Economics, Univ of Wyoming, Box 3354 Univ Station, Laramie WY 82071. 307/766-5124. Through workshops, study guides and media development, Randy specializes in making stress research understandable and usable by lay audiences. His training in human relations and education allows him to tailor programs to the needs of specific audiences. Randy has trained students, faculty, parents, ranchers, farmers and helping professionals in stress management.

Genie L Wessel, RN, MS, FASHA. Administrative Specialist of Health Education, Frederick County Public Schools Health Services, 115 E Church St, Frederick MD 21701. 301/694-2156. Genie is now working to promote wellness in a large school system. She continues to share expertise in stress management and writing. She has been a founder and planner for the Maryland State Wellness Conference.

FUTURE CONTRIBUTORS

If you have developed an exciting, effective structured exercise you'd like to share with other trainers in the field of stress or wellness, please send it to us for consideration, using the following guidelines:

- Your entry should be written in a format similar to those in this volume.

- Contributors must either guarantee that the materials they submit are not previously copyrighted or provide a copyright release for inclusion in the Whole Person **Structured Exercises** series.

- When you have adapted the work of others, please acknowledge the original source of ideas or activities.

EDITORS

All exercises in this volume not specifically attributed to other contributors are the creative efforts of the editors, who have been designing, collecting, and experimenting with structured processes in their teaching, training and consultation work since the late 1960s.

Nancy Loving Tubesing, EdD, holds a masters degree in group counseling and a doctorate in counselor education. She served as editor of the *Society for Wholistic Medicine's* monograph series and articulated the principles of whole person health care in the monograph, **Philosophical Assumptions**. Faculty Associate and Product Development Coordinator at Whole Person Associates, Nancy is always busy compiling and testing teaching designs for future **Structured Exercises** volumes.

Donald A Tubesing, MDiv, PhD, designer of the classic **Stress Skills** seminar and author of the best-selling **Kicking Your Stress Habits**, has been a pioneer in the movement to reintegrate body, mind, and spirit in health care delivery. With his entrepreneurial spirit and background in theology, psychology, and education, Don brings the whole person perspective to his writing, speaking, and consultation in business and industry, government agencies, health care and human service systems.

Nancy and Don have collaborated on many writing projects over the years, beginning with a small-group college orientation project in 1970 and including two self-help books on whole person wellness, **The Caring Question** (Minneapolis: Augsburg, 1983) and **Seeking Your Healthy Balance** (Duluth: Whole Person Press, 1991) and a score of unusual relaxation audiotapes.

The Tubesings have specialized in developing creative stress management programs and packages for client groups such as the national YMCA (8-session course, **The Y's Way to Stress Management**) and Aid Association for Lutherans (**The Stress Kit** multimedia resource for families).

Their most recent efforts have been directed toward combining the process-oriented approach of the **Structured Exercises** series with the power of video. The resulting three six-session interactive video courses, **WellAware**, **Manage It!**, and **Managing Job Stress**, include participant booklets with worksheets that stimulate personal reflection and application of principles to specific situations, as well as a step-by-step leader manual for guiding group interaction.

©1994 Whole Person Press 210 W Michigan Duluth MN 55802   (800) 247-6789

WORKSHOPS-IN-A-BOOK

KICKING YOUR STRESS HABITS:
A Do-it-yourself Guide to Coping with Stress
Donald A. Tubesing, PhD

Over a quarter of a million people have found ways to deal with their everyday stress by using **Kicking Your Stress Habits**. This workshop-in-a-book actively involves the reader in assessing stressful patterns and developing more effective coping strategies with helpful "Stop and Reflect" sections in each chapter.

The 10-step planning process and 20 skills for managing stress make **Kicking Your Stress Habits** an ideal text for stress management classes in many different settings, from hospitals to universities and for a wide variety of groups.

❏ **K / Kicking Your Stress Habits / 14.95**

SEEKING YOUR HEALTHY BALANCE:
A Do-it-yourself Guide to Whole Person Well-being
Donald A. Tubesing, PhD and Nancy Loving Tubesing, EdD

Where can you find the time and energy to "do it all" without sacrificing your health and well-being? **Seeking Your Healthy Balance** helps the reader discover how to make changes toward a more balanced lifestyle by learning effective ways to juggle work, self, and others; clarifying self-care options; and discovering and setting their own personal priorities.

Seeking Your Healthy Balance asks the questions and helps readers find their own answers.

❏ **HB / Seeking Your Healthy Balance / 14.95**

©1994 Whole Person Press 210 W Michigan Duluth MN 55802   (800) 247-6789

STRUCTURED EXERCISES
IN STRESS MANAGEMENT—VOLUMES 1-4
Nancy Loving Tubesing, EdD and Donald A. Tubesing, PhD, Editors

Each book in this four-volume series contains 36 ready-to-use teaching modules that involve the participant—as a whole person—in learning how to manage stress more effectively.

Each exercise is carefully designed by top stress-management professionals. Instructions are clearly written and field-tested so that even beginning trainers can smoothly lead a group through warm-up and closure, reflection and planning, and action and interaction—all with minimum preparation time.

Each Stress Handbook is brimming with practical ideas that you can weave into your own teaching designs or mix and match to develop new programs for varied settings, audiences, and time frames. In each volume you'll find **Icebreakers, Stress Assessments, Management Strategies, Skill Builders, Action Planners, Closing Processes** and **Group Energizers**—all with a special focus on stress management.

STRUCTURED EXERCISES
IN WELLNESS PROMOTION—VOLUMES 1-4
Nancy Loving Tubesing, EdD and Donald A. Tubesing, PhD, Editors

Discover the Wellness Handbooks—from the wellness pioneers at Whole Person Associates. Each volume in this innovative series includes 36 experiential learning activities that focus on whole person health—body, mind, spirit, emotions, relationships, and lifestyle.

The exercises, developed by an interdisciplinary pool of leaders in the wellness movement nationwide, actively encourage people to adopt wellness-oriented attitudes and to develop more responsible self-care patterns.

All process designs in the Wellness Handbooks are clearly explained and have been thoroughly field-tested with diverse audiences so that trainers can use them with confidence. **Icebreakers, Wellness Explorations, Self-Care Strategies, Action Planners, Closings** and **Group Energizers** are all ready-to-go—including reproducible worksheets, scripts, and chalktalk outlines—for the busy professional who wants to develop unique wellness programs without spending oodles of time in preparation.

STRUCTURED EXERCISES IN STRESS AND WELLNESS ARE AVAILABLE IN TWO FORMATS

LOOSE-LEAF FORMAT (8 1/2" x 11")

The loose-leaf, 3-ring binder format provides you with maximum flexiblity. The binder gives you plenty of room to add your own adaptations, workshop outlines, or notes right where you need them. The index tabs offer quick and easy access to each section of exercises, and the generous margins allow plenty of room for notes. In addition an extra set of the full-size worksheets and handouts are packaged separately for convenient duplication.

SOFTCOVER FORMAT (6" x 9")

The softcover format is a perfect companion to the loose-leaf version. This smaller book fits easily into your briefcase or bag, and the binding has been designed to remain open on your desk or lecturn. Worksheets and handouts can be enlarged and photocopied for distribution to your participants, or you can purchase sets of worksheet masters.

WORKSHEET MASTERS

The Worksheet Masters for the two Structured Exercise series offer full-size (8 1/2" x 11") photocopy masters. All of the worksheets and handouts for each volume are reproduced in easy-to-read print with professional graphics. All you need to do to complete your workshop preparation is run them through a copier.

Structured Exercises in Stress Management

- ❑ Loose-Leaf Edition—Volume 1-4 / $54.95 each
- ❑ Softcover Edition—Volume 1-4 / $29.95 each
- ❑ Worksheet Masters—Volume 1-4 / $9.95 each

Structured Exercises in Wellness Promotion

- ❑ Loose-Leaf Edition—Volume 1-4 / $54.95 each
- ❑ Softcover Edition—Volume 1-4 / $29.95 each
- ❑ Worksheet Masters—Volume 1-4 / $9.95 each

ADDITIONAL GROUP PROCESS RESOURCES

Our group process exercises are designed to address the whole person—physical, emotional, mental, spiritual, and social. Developed for trainers by trainers, all of these group process resources are ready-to-use. The novice trainer will find everything they need to get started, and the expert trainer will discover new ideas and concepts to add to their existing programs.

All of the exercises encourage interaction between the leader and the participants, as well as among the participants. Each exercise includes everything you need to present a meaningful program: goals, optimal group size, time frame, materials list, and the complete process instructions.

PLAYFUL ACTIVITIES FOR POWERFUL PRESENTATIONS
Bruce Williamson

This book contains 40 fun exercises designed to fit any group or topic. These exercises will help you:

- build teamwork
- encourage laughter and playfulness
- relieve stress and tension
- free up the imaginations of participants

   ❑ **PAP / Playful Activities for Powerful Presentations / $19.95**

WORKING WITH GROUPS FROM DYSFUNCTIONAL FAMILIES
Cheryl Hetherington

This collection of 29 proven group activities is designed to heal the pain that results from growing up in or living in a dysfunctional family. With these exercises you can:

- promote healing
- build self-esteem
- encourage sharing
- help participants acknowledge their feelings

WORKING WITH GROUPS FROM DYSFUNCTIONAL FAMILIES REPRODUCIBLE WORKSHEET MASTERS

A complete package of full-size (8 1/2" x 11") photocopy masters that include all the worksheets and handouts from **Working with Groups from Dysfunctional Families** is available to you. Use the masters for easy duplication of the handouts for each participant.

   ❑ **DFH / Working with Groups from Dysfunctional Families / $19.95**
   ❑ **DFW / Dysfunctional Families Worksheet Masters / $9.95**

WORKING WITH WOMEN'S GROUPS Volumes 1 & 2
Louise Yolton Eberhardt

The two volumes of **Working with Women's Groups** have been completely revised and updated. These exercises will help women explore issues that are of perennial concern as well as today's hot topics.

- consciousness-raising (volume 1)
- self-discovery (volume 1)
- assertiveness training (volume 1)
- sexuality issues (volume 2)
- women of color (volume 2)
- leadership skills training (volume 2)

> ❏ **WG1 / Working with Women's Groups—Volume 1 / $19.95**
> ❏ **WG2 / Working with Women's Groups—Volume 2 / $19.95**

WORKING WITH MEN'S GROUPS
Roger Karsk and Bill Thomas

Also revised and updated, this volume is a valuable resource for anyone working with men's groups. The exercises cover a variety of topics, including:

- self discovery
- parenting
- conflict
- intimacy

> ❏ **MG / Working with Men's Groups / $19.95**

WELLNESS ACTIVITIES FOR YOUTH Volumes 1 & 2
Sandy Queen

Each volume of **Wellness Activities for Youth** helps leaders teach children and teenagers about wellness with an emphasis on FUN. The concepts include:

- values
- stress and coping
- self-esteem
- personal well-being

WELLNESS ACTIVITIES FOR YOUTH WORKSHEET MASTERS

Complete packages of full-size (8 1/2" x 11") photocopy masters that include all the worksheets and handouts from **Wellness Activities for Youth Volumes 1 and 2** are available to you. Use the masters for easy duplication of the handouts for each participant.

> ❏ **WY1 / Wellness Activities for Youth Volume 1 / $19.95**
> ❏ **WY2 / Wellness Activities for Youth Volume 2 / $19.95**
> ❏ **WY1W / Wellness Activities for Youth V.1 Worksheet Masters / $9.95**
> ❏ **WY2W / Wellness Activities for Youth V. 2 Worksheet Masters / $9.95**

RELAXATION AUDIOTAPES

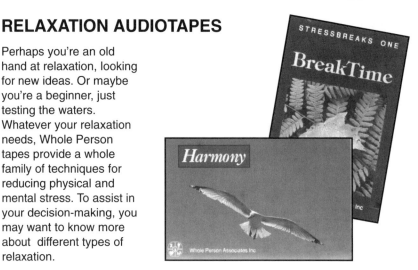

Perhaps you're an old hand at relaxation, looking for new ideas. Or maybe you're a beginner, just testing the waters. Whatever your relaxation needs, Whole Person tapes provide a whole family of techniques for reducing physical and mental stress. To assist in your decision-making, you may want to know more about different types of relaxation.

We offer six different types of relaxation techniques in our twenty-one tapes. The Whole Person series ranges from simple breathing and stretching exercises, to classic autogenic and progressive relaxation sequences, to guided meditations and whimsical daydreams. All are carefully crafted to promote whole person relaxation—body, mind, and spirit. We also provide a line of music-only tapes, composed specifically for relaxation.

SENSATIONAL RELAXATION

When stress piles up, it becomes a heavy load both physically and emotionally. These full-length relaxation experiences will teach you techniques that can be used whenever you feel that stress is getting out of control. Choose one you like and repeat it daily until it becomes second nature then recall that technique whenever you need it.

> ❑ **CD / Countdown to Relaxation / $9.95**
> ❑ **DS / Daybreak / Sundown / $9.95**
> ❑ **TDB / Take a Deep Breath / $9.95**
> ❑ **RLX / Relax . . . Let Go . . . Relax / $9.95**
> ❑ **SRL / StressRelease / $9.95**
> ❑ **WRM / Warm and Heavy / $9.95**

STRESS BREAKS

Do you need a short energy booster or a quick stress reliever? If you don't know what type of relaxation you like, or if you are new to guided relaxation techniques, try one of our Stress Breaks for a quick refocusing or change of pace any time of the day.

> ❑ **BT / BreakTime / $9.95**
> ❑ **NT / Natural Tranquilizers / $9.95**

DAYDREAMS

Escape from the stress around you with guided tours to beautiful places. Picture yourself traveling to the ocean, sitting in a park, luxuriating in the view from the majestic mountains, or enjoying the solitude and serenity of a cozy cabin. The 10-minute escapes included in our Daydream tapes will lead your imagination away from your everyday cares so you can resume your tasks relaxed and comforted.

- ❏ **DD1 / Daydreams 1: Getaways / $9.95**
- ❏ **DD2 / Daydreams 2: Peaceful Places / $9.95**

GUIDED MEDITATION

Take a step beyond relaxation and discover the connection between body and mind with guided meditation. The imagery in our full-length meditations will help you discover your strengths, find healing, make positive life changes, and recognize your inner wisdom.

- ❏ **IH / Inner Healing / $9.95**
- ❏ **PE / Personal Empowering / $9.95**
- ❏ **HBT / Healthy Balancing / $9.95**
- ❏ **SPC / Spiritual Centering / $9.95**

WILDERNESS DAYDREAMS

Discover the healing power of nature with the four tapes in the Wilderness Daydreams series. The eight special journeys will transport you from your harried, stressful surroundings to the peaceful serenity of words and water.

- ❏ **WD1 / Canoe / Rain / $9.95**
- ❏ **WD2 / Island /Spring / $9.95**
- ❏ **WD3 / Campfire / Stream / $9.95**
- ❏ **WD4 / Sailboat / Pond / $9.95**

MUSIC ONLY

No relaxation program would be complete without relaxing melodies that can be played as background to a prepared script or that can be enjoyed as you practice a technique you have already learned. Steven Eckels composed his melodies specifically for relaxation. These "musical prayers for healing" will calm your body, mind, and spirit.

- ❏ **T / Tranquility / $9.95**
- ❏ **H / Harmony / $9.95**
- ❏ **S / Serenity / $9.95**

Titles can be combined for discounts!

QUANTITY DISCOUNT			
1 - 9	10 - 49	50 - 99	100+
$9.95	$8.95	$7.96	CALL

©1994 Whole Person Press 210 W Michigan Duluth MN 55802 (800) 247-6789

RELAXATION RESOURCES

Many trainers and workshop leaders have discovered the benefits of relaxation and visualization in healing the body, mind, and spirit.

30 SCRIPTS FOR RELAXATION, IMAGERY, AND INNER HEALING
Julie Lusk

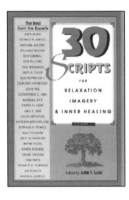

These two volumes are collections of relaxation scripts created by trainers for trainers. The 30 scripts in each of the two volumes have been professionally-tested and fine-tuned so they are ready to use for both novice and expert trainers.

Help your participants change their behavior, enhance their self-esteem, discover inner, private places, and heal themselves through simple trainer-led guided imagery scripts. Both volumes include information on how to use the scripts, suggestions for tailoring them to your specific needs and audience, and information on how to successfully incorporate guided imagery into your existing programs.

❏ **30S / 30 Scripts for Relaxation, Imagery, and Inner Healing—Volume 1 / $19.95**
❏ **30S2 / 30 Scripts for Relaxation, Imagery, and Inner Healing—Volume 2 / $19.95**

INQUIRE WITHIN
Andrew Schwartz

Use visualization to make positive changes in your life. The 24 visualization experiences in **Inquire Within** will help participants enhance their creativity, heal inner pain, learn to relax, and deal with conflict. Each visualization includes questions at the end of the process that encourage deeper reflection and a better understanding of the exercise and the response it invokes.

❏ **IW / Inquire Within / $19.95**

©1994 Whole Person Press 210 W Michigan Duluth MN 55802   (800) 247-6789

ORDER FORM

Name _____

Address _____

City _____

State/Zip _____

Area Code/Telephone _____

Please make checks payable to:
Whole Person Associates Inc
210 West Michigan
Duluth MN 55802-1908
FAX: 1-218-727-0505
TOLL FREE: 1-800-247-6789

Books / Workshops-In-A-Book
___ Kicking Your Stress Habits .... $14.95 _____
___ Seeking Your Healthy Balance .... $14.95 _____

Structured Exercises in Stress Management Series—Volumes 1-4
___ Stress Softcover Edition .... Vol 1 ___ Vol 2 ___ Vol 3 ___ Vol 4 ___ $29.95 _____
___ Stress Loose-Leaf Edition .... Vol 1 ___ Vol 2 ___ Vol 3 ___ Vol 4 ___ $54.95 _____
___ Stress Worksheets Masters .... Vol 1 ___ Vol 2 ___ Vol 3 ___ Vol 4 ___ $9.95 _____

Structured Exercises in Wellness Promotion Series—Volumes 1-4
___ Wellness Softcover Edition .... Vol 1 ___ Vol 2 ___ Vol 3 ___ Vol 4 ___ $29.95 _____
___ Wellness Loose-Leaf Edition .... Vol 1 ___ Vol 2 ___ Vol 3 ___ Vol 4 ___ $54.95 _____
___ Wellness Worksheets Masters ...... Vol 1 ___ Vol 2 ___ Vol 3 ___ Vol 4 ___ $9.95 _____

Group Process Resources
___ Playful Activities for Powerful Presentations .... $19.95 _____
___ Working with Groups from Dysfunctional Families .... $19.95 _____
___ Working with Groups from Dysfunctional Families Worksheet Masters .... $ 9.95 _____
___ Working with Women's Groups .... Vol 1 ___ Vol 2 ___ $19.95 _____
___ Working with Men's Groups .... $19.95 _____
___ Wellness Activities for Youth .... Vol 1 ___ Vol 2 ___ $19.95 _____
___ Wellness Activities for Youth Worksheet Master .... Vol 1 ___ Vol 2 ___ $9.95 _____

Relaxation Audiotapes
___ BreakTime .... $ 9.95 _____
___ Countdown to Relaxation .... $ 9.95 _____
___ Daybreak/Sundown .... $ 9.95 _____
___ Daydreams 1: Getaways .... $ 9.95 _____
___ Daydreams 2: Peaceful Places .... $ 9.95 _____
___ Harmony (music only) .... $ 9.95 _____
___ Healthy Balancing .... $ 9.95 _____
___ Inner Healing .... $ 9.95 _____
___ Natural Tranquilizers .... $ 9.95 _____
___ Personal Empowering .... $ 9.95 _____
___ Relax . . . Let Go . . . Relax .... $ 9.95 _____
___ Serenity (music only) .... $ 9.95 _____
___ Spiritual Centering .... $ 9.95 _____
___ StressRelease .... $ 9.95 _____
___ Take a Deep Breath .... $ 9.95 _____
___ Tranquility (music only) .... $ 9.95 _____
___ Warm and Heavy .... $ 9.95 _____
___ Wilderness DD 1: Canoe/Rain .... $ 9.95 _____
___ Wilderness DD 2: Island/Spring .... $ 9.95 _____
___ Wilderness DD 3: Campfire/Stream .... $ 9.95 _____
___ Wilderness DD 4: Sailboat/Pond .... $ 9.95 _____

Relaxation Resources
___ 30 Scripts—Volume 1 .... $19.95 _____
___ 30 Scripts—Volume 2 .... $19.95 _____
___ Inquire Within .... $19.95 _____

My check is enclosed. **(US funds only)**
Please charge my _____ Visa _____ Mastercard
_____
Exp date _____
Signature _____

SUBTOTAL	_____
TAX (MN residents 6.5%)	_____
7% GST-Canadian customers only	_____
**SHIPPING*	_____
GRAND TOTAL	_____

800-247-6789

** **SHIPPING**. $5.00 ($8.00 outside U.S.)
Please call us for quotes on UPS 3rd Day,
2nd Day or Next Day Air.

ORDER FORM

Name _____

Address _____

City _____

State/Zip _____

Area Code/Telephone _____

Please make checks payable to:
Whole Person Associates Inc
210 West Michigan
Duluth MN 55802-1908
FAX: 1-218-727-0505
TOLL FREE: 1-800-247-6789

Books / Workshops-In-A-Book
____ Kicking Your Stress Habits .... $14.95 _____
____ Seeking Your Healthy Balance .... $14.95 _____

Structured Exercises in Stress Management Series—Volumes 1-4
____ Stress Softcover Edition .... Vol 1 ___ Vol 2 ___ Vol 3 ___ Vol 4 ___ $29.95 _____
____ Stress Loose-Leaf Edition .... Vol 1 ___ Vol 2 ___ Vol 3 ___ Vol 4 ___ $54.95 _____
____ Stress Worksheets Masters .... Vol 1 ___ Vol 2 ___ Vol 3 ___ Vol 4 ___ $9.95 _____

Structured Exercises in Wellness Promotion Series—Volumes 1-4
____ Wellness Softcover Edition .... Vol 1 ___ Vol 2 ___ Vol 3 ___ Vol 4 ___ $29.95 _____
____ Wellness Loose-Leaf Edition .... Vol 1 ___ Vol 2 ___ Vol 3 ___ Vol 4 ___ $54.95 _____
____ Wellness Worksheets Masters .... Vol 1 ___ Vol 2 ___ Vol 3 ___ Vol 4 ___ $9.95 _____

Group Process Resources
____ Playful Activities for Powerful Presentations .... $19.95 _____
____ Working with Groups from Dysfunctional Families .... $19.95 _____
____ Working with Groups from Dysfunctional Families Worksheet Masters .... $ 9.95 _____
____ Working with Women's Groups .... Vol 1 ___ Vol 2 ___ $19.95 _____
____ Working with Men's Groups .... $19.95 _____
____ Wellness Activities for Youth .... Vol 1 ___ Vol 2 ___ $19.95 _____
____ Wellness Activities for Youth Worksheet Master .... Vol 1 ___ Vol 2 ___ $9.95 _____

Relaxation Audiotapes
____ BreakTime .... $ 9.95 _____
____ Countdown to Relaxation .... $ 9.95 _____
____ Daybreak/Sundown .... $ 9.95 _____
____ Daydreams 1: Getaways .... $ 9.95 _____
____ Daydreams 2: Peaceful Places .... $ 9.95 _____
____ Harmony (music only) .... $ 9.95 _____
____ Healthy Balancing .... $ 9.95 _____
____ Inner Healing .... $ 9.95 _____
____ Natural Tranquilizers .... $ 9.95 _____
____ Personal Empowering .... $ 9.95 _____
____ Relax . . . Let Go . . . Relax .... $ 9.95 _____
____ Serenity (music only) .... $ 9.95 _____
____ Spiritual Centering .... $ 9.95 _____
____ StressRelease .... $ 9.95 _____
____ Take a Deep Breath .... $ 9.95 _____
____ Tranquility (music only) .... $ 9.95 _____
____ Warm and Heavy .... $ 9.95 _____
____ Wilderness DD 1: Canoe/Rain .... $ 9.95 _____
____ Wilderness DD 2: Island/Spring .... $ 9.95 _____
____ Wilderness DD 3: Campfire/Stream .... $ 9.95 _____
____ Wilderness DD 4: Sailboat/Pond .... $ 9.95 _____

Relaxation Resources
____ 30 Scripts—Volume 1 .... $19.95 _____
____ 30 Scripts—Volume 2 .... $19.95 _____
____ Inquire Within .... $19.95 _____

My check is enclosed. **(US funds only)**
Please charge my _____ Visa _____ Mastercard
_____
Exp date _____
Signature _____

SUBTOTAL _____
TAX (MN residents 6.5%) _____
7% GST-Canadian customers only _____
***SHIPPING** _____
GRAND TOTAL _____

800-247-6789

** **SHIPPING**. $5.00 ($8.00 outside U.S.)
Please call us for quotes on UPS 3rd Day,
2nd Day or Next Day Air.

About Whole Person Associates

At Whole Person Associates, we're 100% committed to providing stress and wellness materials that involve participants and have a "whole person" focus—body, mind, spirit, and relationships.

That's our mission and it's very important to us—but it doesn't tell the whole story. Behind the products in our catalog is a company full of people—and *that's* what really makes us who we are.

ABOUT THE OWNERS

Whole Person Associates was created by the vision of two people: Donald A. Tubesing, PhD, and Nancy Loving Tubesing, EdD. Since way back in 1970, Don and Nancy have been active in the stress management / wellness movement—consulting, leading seminars, writing, and publishing. Most of our early products were the result of their creativity and expertise.

Living proof that you can "stay evergreen," Don and Nancy remain the driving force behind the company and are still very active in developing new products that touch people's lives.

ABOUT THE COMPANY

Whole Person Associates was "born" in Duluth, Minnesota, and we remain committed to our lovely city on the shore of Lake Superior. All of our operations are here, which makes communication between departments much easier!

We've grown since our beginnings, but at a steady pace—we're interested in sustainable growth that allows us to keep our down-to-earth orientation—and put the same high quality into every product we offer.

ABOUT OUR EMPLOYEES

Speaking of down-to-earth, that's a requirement for each and every one of our employees. We're all product consultants, which means that anyone who answers the phone can probably answer your questions (if they can't, they'll find someone who can.)

We focus on helping you find the products that fit your needs. And we've found that the best way to do that is to hire friendly and resourceful people.

ABOUT OUR ASSOCIATES

Who are the "associates" in Whole Person Associates? They're the trainers, authors, musicians, and others who have developed much of the material you see on these pages. We're always on the lookout for high-quality products that reflect our "whole person" philosophy and fill a need for our customers.

Most of our products were developed by experts who are the tops in their fields, and we're very proud to be associated with them.

ABOUT OUR CUSTOMERS

Finally, we wouldn't have a reason to exist without you, our customers. We've met some of you, and we've talked to many more of you on the phone. We are always aware that without you, there would be no Whole Person Associates.

That's why we'd love to hear from you! Let us know what you think of our products—how you use them in your work, what additional products you'd like to see, and what shortcomings you've noted. Write us or call on our toll-free line. We're waiting for your call!

©1994 Whole Person Press 210 W Michigan Duluth MN 55802   (800) 247-6789